INTRODUCTION

Whether you live on your own or you have a family, every night a meal has to be provided. We don't all want to rely on convenience foods or resort to eating out, so it often becomes a problem choosing what to cook. It really needs to be quick and easy, guaranteed to work and not cost a fortune. Then of course there are the occasions when you want a special meal for a dinner party or as a treat. This book will help you solve all these problems. Beautifully illustrated with large colour photographs and step by steps, showing clearly all the skills and techniques involved, there are a range of ideas for you to choose from.

When time is short why not try tender succulent Noisettes of Lamb or Pork Escalopes, or if you're watching the pennies try all-time favourites, Shepherd's Pie and Steak and Mushroom Puddings, guaranteed to satisfy the heartiest appetite or a quick and easy Spaghetti Bolognese. Then when you're out to impress, there's a host of ideas to stimulate your palate, ranging from Crown Roast of Lamb, Individual Beef Wellingtons to Roast Duck with Orange.

This collection of recipes would not be complete without some good old English favourites, like Roast Chicken, Roast Beef or Golden Fish Pie.

Whichever recipe you try you can cook it with confidence as every single recipe has been thoroughly tested in the Woman's Own Test Kitchen to guarantee a perfect result every time and to ensure that the recipe tastes as good as it looks.

I hope you enjoy the book.

Happy cooking

Gina Steer

Gina Steer

CORONATION CHICKEN

Succulent pieces of chicken, toasted almonds and sweet, sun-ripened apricots with a delicately flavoured mayonnaise make this dish delicious for any occasion. Serve with a green salad and new potatoes.

3½ lb/1.5 kg oven-ready free-range chicken

2 onions, peeled

1 carrot, peeled

4 cloves

1 stick celery trimmed

few thyme sprigs

few parsley sprigs

4 bay leaves

1 tbsp oil

1 level tbsp curry powder

1½ tbsp tomato purée

¼ pint/150 ml white wine or wine and water mixed together

2 lemon slices

juice of ½ lemon

¼ pint/150 ml fromage frais

¼ pint/150 ml reduced-calorie mayonnaise

14 oz/397 g can apricots, drained

2 oz/50 g blanched almonds, toasted

4 oz/100 g no-need-to-soak dried apricots

1 ripe nectarine

salad leaves

Wash chicken thoroughly, discarding any giblets. Place chicken in a large flameproof casserole and cover with water. Add one of the peeled onions, the carrot and cloves. Cut the celery stick in half and place the thyme, parsley and 2 of bay leaves over one half. Tie the other half of celery over top to make a bouquet garni. Add to the pan. Bring to boil, cover, reduce heat and poach the chicken for 1½-2 hrs or until cooked. Cool slightly then remove from pan, drain and leave covered until cold. Strip off and discard the skin. Remove the chicken meat from the carcass and cut into small cubes. Cover while making sauce.

Heat oil in a small pan, chop the remaining onion. Fry the onion in the oil for 5 mins, add the 2 remaining bay leaves and curry powder, and continue to cook for 3 mins. Add the tomato purée, wine or water and wine with the lemon slices and lemon juice, simmer gently for 10 mins then strain and reserve the liquid.

Mix the fromage frais and the mayonnaise together, then stir in the cooled liquid. Purée the canned apricots, then stir into the curry mayonnaise with seasoning. Add the cubed chicken with 1½ oz/40 g of the almonds. Chop the dried apricots and add to the chicken mixture. Stir until all the ingredients are lightly coated. Stone the nectarine and cut into thin slices. Arrange salad leaves on serving dish then spoon the chicken into the dish. Decorate with the sliced nectarine and scatter remaining almonds on top.

HANDY TIPS

If preferred you can use cashew nuts instead of the blanched almonds and you can replace the nectarine with a peach.

1. Poach the chicken with the onion, carrot, cloves and bouquet garni

2. When cold, strip off the skin, remove meat from the carcass and cube

3. Fry onion for 5 mins, add bay leaves and curry powder, and cook for 3 mins

4. Strain the sauce into a bowl. Set aside and allow the liquid to cool

5. Purée the canned apricots and then stir into the curry mayonnaise

6. Stir chicken into mayonnaise with almonds and apricots until coated

CHICKEN KORMA

Tender chicken in a rich, creamy yogurt sauce, delicately flavoured with coriander and just the merest hint of spices, make this an excellent dish to give the whole family for an extra-special treat from the East.

Calories per portion: 407

SERVES 4

3½ lb/1.5 kg oven-ready
   free-range chicken
1 tsp turmeric
1 tsp salt
10 green cardamom pods
4 tbsp ghee, or sunflower oil
2 onions, peeled and chopped
2 in/5 cm piece of root ginger
5 garlic cloves, peeled
   and crushed
5 cloves
1 cinnamon stick
¼ - ½ tsp freshly grated nutmeg
1 oz/25 g ground almonds
1 pint/600 ml natural yogurt
freshly ground black pepper
2 tbsp freshly chopped coriander
1 tbsp lemon juice

Wash chicken, then cut into eight pieces – discarding the parson's nose, the scale ends of the drumsticks, and the neck flap. Wash again, then place in a large pan with 1½ pints/900 ml water, ½ tsp turmeric, salt and 7 cardamom pods. Bring to the boil, cover, then reduce the heat and simmer gently for 45 mins, or until the chicken is tender. Then remove chicken, reserving the stock, and allow to cool slightly. Finally, skin the chicken pieces and keep

covered while preparing the sauce.

Meanwhile, heat the ghee or oil in a large frying pan, add the onions and fry for 10-15 mins, stirring frequently, until golden. Remove from the pan using a slotted spoon, then drain on kitchen paper and reserve. Peel and finely chop the ginger, then add to the frying pan together with the crushed garlic, remaining turmeric, cloves, cinnamon stick, remaining cardamom pods and the grated nutmeg. Continue to fry the spices for 5 mins, then stir in the ground almonds.

Add the yogurt and ¼ pint/150 ml reserved chicken stock and bring to a gentle simmer. Cook for 15 mins or until the mixture has reduced and is of a thick consistency. Return the onions to the pan, together with the chicken pieces and a further ¼ pint/150 ml chicken stock. Ensure the chicken is well coated with the sauce, then cover the pan and cook for 15-20 mins, or until chicken is piping hot. Add the freshly ground black pepper to taste, then stir in the coriander and lemon juice. Heat for a further 5 mins, stir to ensure the flavours are thoroughly distributed. Serve with freshly cooked rice, salad and poppadoms.

HANDY TIPS

The whole spices are not meant to be eaten but should be left to one side. If there is a lot of oil floating around the edge of the sauce, spoon off and discard.

1. Cut chicken into eight pieces, place in pan with 1½ pints/900 ml water and spices

2. Fry onions until golden brown, stirring frequently, then drain and reserve

3. Add ginger, garlic and remaining spices to the pan and fry for 5 mins

MAIN COURSES

MAIN COURSES

Classic step-by-step Cookery Collection

GINA STEER

COOKERY EDITOR OF WOMAN'S OWN

HAMLYN

CONTENTS

First published 1992
Hamlyn is an imprint of
Octopus Illustrated Publishing,
part of Reed International Books Limited,
Michelin House, 81 Fulham Road,
London, SW3 6RB

Text and illustrations © 1992 IPC
Magazines Limited
Design © 1992 Reed International
Books Limited

A catalogue record for this book is
available from the British Library

ISBN 0 600 57563 2

Produced by Mandarin Offset
Printed and Bound in Hong Kong

NOTES

Both metric and imperial measurements have been used in all recipes.
Use one set of measurements only and not a mixture of both.

Standard level spoon measurements are used in all recipes
1 tablespoon = one 15 ml spoon
1 teaspoon = one 5 ml spoon

Ovens should be preheated to the specific temperature.
If using a fan assisted oven, follow manufacturer's instructions
for adjusting the temperature.

4. Add ground almonds, yogurt and stock and cook for 15 mins, then stir in onions

5. Add the chicken to the pan, then stir in a further ¼ pint/150 ml reserved stock

6. Add the black pepper, then sprinkle in chopped coriander and lemon juice

CHICKEN KIEV

The joy of this delicious dish is actually found inside the chicken. Cut into it and you release a river of mouthwatering garlic butter which has melted, filling the meat with its distinctive flavour. Easy to make and perfect for a special treat.

Calories per portion: 708　　　　　　　　　　　　　　　　　**SERVES 4**

4 large chicken breasts
6 oz/175 g butter
salt and freshly ground
    black pepper
2 tbsp freshly chopped parsley
1 garlic clove, peeled and crushed
1 egg, size 1, beaten
8 oz/225 g fresh white
    breadcrumbs
oil for deep frying

Remove the bones from the chicken breasts, using a very sharp knife, leaving as much meat as possible intact. Remove the skin from each chicken breast by grasping the skin firmly between forefinger and thumb and carefully pulling away from flesh. Using either a meat mallet or rolling pin, beat each chicken breast until flattened to about ¼ in/6 mm thick. (You may find this easier if you place the meat between sheets of greaseproof paper or clearwrap first.)

Place the butter in a small bowl and cream with a spoon until softened. Add plenty of seasoning, the chopped parsley and crushed garlic. Mix well. Divide the butter into four, place each portion on a sheet of greaseproof paper and roll into a barrel shape in the paper. Wrap in greaseproof paper and chill well for about 30 mins.

Discard the paper from the chicken and butter. Season the chicken on all sides and place a barrel of butter in the centre of each piece, boned side up, then fold the chicken around the butter, tucking the sides in to encase it. Secure each chicken parcel with a cocktail stick.

Dip the parcels in the beaten egg and then coat in the breadcrumbs. Repeat coating to ensure that all the chicken is covered by a layer of breadcrumbs.

Heat oil in a large saucepan or electric deep-fat fryer until a cube of bread added to the oil rises to the surface immediately surrounded by bubbles. Carefully add two of the Chicken Kievs and fry for 6-8 mins until crisp and golden. Remove from oil and drain well on kitchen paper. Fry and drain remaining kievs. Remove cocktail sticks and serve while hot.

HANDY TIPS

For a healthy version use fresh wholemeal breadcrumbs and use sunflower oil for frying or lightly brush the base of a roasting tin, add the prepared Kievs then cook in the oven at Gas 5, 375°F, 190°C, for 30-40 mins.

1. Using a very sharp knife, carefully remove bones from the chicken

2. Grasp the skin firmly and pull carefully away from the flesh

3. Flatten each of the four chicken breasts with a meat mallet

4. Roll each quarter of the butter into a barrel shape and chill

5. Place the butter on each portion of chicken and fold over

6. Dip the chicken parcels into the egg and then into the breadcrumbs

CHICKEN & LEEK PIE

Poached chicken, lightly sautéed with shallots and leeks in a home-made chicken sauce, topped with a golden pastry. This Chicken & Leek Pie is a real family treat and so easy to make; just follow the easy step-by-step guide.

Calories per portion: 833   **SERVES 6**

3½ lb/1.5 kg oven-ready
    free-range chicken
2 large onions
2 carrots
2 sticks celery
2 bay leaves
4-6 black peppercorns
4 cloves
2 oz/50 g butter or margarine
12 oz/350 g leeks, trimmed,
    washed and sliced
8 oz/225 g shallots, peeled
FOR THE SAUCE:
2 oz/50 g butter or margarine
2 oz/50 g plain flour
FOR THE PASTRY:
4 oz/100 g white vegetable fat
2 oz/50 g butter or margarine
10 oz/300 g plain flour
1 egg, size 5, beaten

Preheat oven to Gas 6, 400°F, 200°C, 15 mins before baking the pie.

Remove any giblets from the chicken. Pull away and discard any fat from the inside of the bird then wash thoroughly under cold running water. Drain then place in a large saucepan. Peel the onions and carrots, trim and scrub the celery. Place in the pan with the bay leaves, peppercorns and cloves. Cover with water. Bring to the boil, cover with lid then reduce heat and simmer for 1½-2 hrs or until chicken is cooked.

Remove chicken from pan, cover and allow to cool. Strain stock and reserve 1 pint/600 ml. (The rest of the stock can be frozen for later use or stored in the fridge, covered, for 2 days.)

When the chicken is cool enough to handle, strip off meat, discarding skin and bones, chop meat into bite-sized pieces, cover and leave on one side.

Melt the butter or margarine then fry the leeks for 5 mins. Drain and reserve. Fry the shallots in the remaining fat for 5 mins or until golden, drain. To make the sauce, melt 2 oz/50 g butter or margarine in a clean pan then stir in

flour and cook for 2 mins over a gentle heat. Remove from heat, stir in the reserved 1 pint/600 ml of chicken stock, return to the heat and cook, stirring throughout until thickened. Add the chicken meat, shallots and leeks with seasoning to taste. Place filling in a 1½ pint/900 ml oval pie dish.

To make the pastry, rub the fats into the flour then mix to a soft pliable

dough with cold water. Knead until smooth, wrap and chill for 30 mins. Roll out on a lightly floured surface and cut out a ½ in/1.25 cm strip, long enough to go all the way round the pie dish. Dampen edge of pie dish and place in position.

Cut out pastry lid as illustrated (in step 4), dampen pastry strip and place the lid on top, sealing the edges firmly together. Knock the edges together with the back of a round-bladed knife. Using your thumb and forefinger, pinch the edges together to form a decorative pattern around the edge of the dish and use the trimmings to decorate the top.

Make a small hole in the centre of the pastry lid to allow the steam to escape. Brush the pie lightly with the beaten egg then cook in the oven for 35-40 mins or until the pastry is golden. Serve hot with a selection of fresh seasonal vegetables.

HANDY TIP

A golden crust is achieved by lightly brushing the pastry with the beaten egg halfway through the cooking time as well as just before baking the pie.

1. *Place the chicken, onions, carrots, celery and bay leaves in a saucepan*

2. *Sauté leeks in fat for 5 mins, then drain. Add shallots to pan and sauté*

3. *Melt fat in saucepan, add flour, cook for 2 mins. Stir in chicken stock*

4. *Roll pastry out on a floured surface to ½ in/1.25 cm thick. Cut oval for lid*

5. *After placing filling in dish, place strip around edge, dampen, position lid*

6. *Seal edges together firmly. Arrange pastry leaves as decoration in centre*

CHICKEN IN A BRICK

Chicken is always a real favourite, any time. But cooked in this special mouth-watering way, with wine, herbs and vegetables, it's extra tender, making a doubly delicious family treat.

Calories per portion: 504   SERVES 4

6 oz/175g shallots

6 oz/175g baby turnips

6 oz/175 g carrots

2 celery sticks

3½ lb/1.5 kg oven-ready
    free-range chicken

1 lemon

4 bay leaves

few fresh tarragon sprigs

salt and freshly ground
    black pepper

¼ pint/150 ml dry white wine

¼ pint/150 ml chicken stock

1 oz/25 g butter or margarine

1 oz/25 g plain flour

2-3 tbsp cream

Preheat the oven to Gas 5, 375°F, 190°C, 10 mins before roasting the chicken in a brick. Place both halves of your chicken brick either in a sink or in 2 large bowls. Cover completely with cold water and leave for at least 30 mins. (This ensures the brick does not dry out and crack during cooking.) Drain.

Peel shallots, trim turnips and scrub lightly. Peel carrots, cut into strips. Trim celery, scrub and cut into chunky pieces. Wash chicken thoroughly and dry. Cut lemon into quarters and place

inside chicken cavity, together with a couple of bay leaves and the sprigs of fresh tarragon. Season well with salt and freshly ground black pepper.

Place half the prepared vegetables in the base of the drained chicken brick, then place chicken on top. Arrange remaining vegetables around the chicken, together with the remaining bay leaves. Pour the white wine and stock over, then place lid on top. Roast in the preheated oven for 1½ hrs or until the chicken is cooked. (To test if the meat is done, insert a skewer into the thickest part of the thigh-the juices should run clear.)

Remove chicken brick from the oven, carefully pour off cooking liquid and reserve. Keep chicken and vegetables hot, covered, in the oven, while preparing the sauce.

Place cooking liquid in a small pan and bring to the boil. Cream fat and flour together to make a beurre manié, then drop small amounts into the boiling liquid, whisking continuously. When sauce is thickened, smooth and glossy, draw off the heat, stir in cream, then reheat gently, and season to taste. Serve with the chicken, vegetables, and potatoes, rice or noodles.

HANDY TIP

Try cooking poussins in a chicken brick. Use two prepared birds, proceed as above but cook for 45 mins or until tender.

1. Place the chicken brick in a bowl, cover with cold water and leave for 30 mins

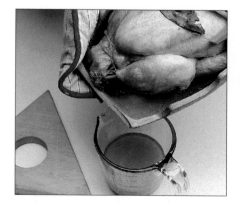

2. Place vegetables, herbs and chicken in brick. Add wine, stock and bay leaves

3. Once chicken is cooked, pour off cooking liquid. Keep chicken and vegetables hot

4. Pour liquid into a small pan and place on the heat. Cream fat and flour together

5. Bring cooking liquid to a gentle boil in a small pan, then drop in small spoonfuls of beurre manié

6. Whisk until the sauce is smooth, season, remove from heat and add the cream

CHICKEN MARYLAND

This tasty American dish is an unusual but mouthwatering combination of golden-coated tender chicken and fried bananas. Served with corn fritters and crispy bacon, it makes a delicious dinner treat that is sure to impress.

Calories per portion: 825   **SERVES 4**

4 chicken quarters, skinned

1 pint/600 ml milk and
    water, mixed

4 oz/100 g plain flour

pinch of white pepper

pinch of cayenne pepper

1 egg, size 3

6 tbsp vegetable oil

FOR THE CORN FRITTERS:

1 egg, size 3, separated

7 oz/200 g can sweetcorn
    kernels, drained

2½ oz/65 g plain flour, sieved

½ tsp baking powder, sieved

salt and freshly ground
    black pepper

oil for deep frying

FOR THE SAUCE:

2 oz/50 g butter or margarine

1 oz/25 g plain flour

¼ pint/150 ml chicken stock

¼ pint/150 ml milk

salt and freshly ground
    black pepper

2 medium bananas

2 tbsp lemon juice

8 rashers streaky bacon,
    derinded

quartered tomatoes and fresh
    herbs to garnish

HANDY TIP

If liked the chicken quarters can be deep fried instead of oven roasted.

Preheat the oven to Gas 4, 350°F, 180°C, 10 mins before cooking. Wash and dry the chicken, then place in a shallow dish. Pour the milk over, cover and chill in the fridge for 30 mins.

Season the flour with the peppers and place on a large plate or in a polythene bag. Beat egg with 2 tbsp water and place in a shallow bowl. Drain the chicken and coat in seasoned flour, dip into beaten egg, then into the flour again. Heat the oil in a frying pan and brown the chicken on both sides. Drain, then place in a roasting tin and roast in the preheated oven for 30-40 mins, or until thoroughly cooked.

To make the corn fritters, beat the egg yolk and the sweetcorn together. Add the flour, baking powder and seasoning. Whisk egg white until stiff, then fold into the corn mixture.

Heat the oil in a deep-fat fryer to 350°F, 180°C. Divide the mixture into 8 then fry fritters in the hot oil for 3-4 mins, or until lightly browned. Drain on kitchen paper.

To make the sauce, melt 1 oz/25 g fat in a saucepan, then stir in the flour and cook for 2 mins. Remove from heat and gradually blend in the stock and milk with seasoning to taste. Return to the heat and stir until thick.

Just before serving, peel the bananas, slice lengthways, then sprinkle with lemon juice. Melt remaining fat in a pan and sauté the bananas and bacon for 3-4 mins or until cooked. Serve with chicken, fritters, sauce and garnish with the quartered tomatoes and herbs.

1. Place chicken quarters in a shallow dish, pour the milk over, cover and chill

2. Drain the chicken, coat in flour, then dip in egg and then into flour again

3. Mix egg yolk and corn. Add flour, baking powder, seasoning and egg white

4. Heat oil to 350°F, 180°C, then fry corn fritters in fryer for 3-4 mins

5. Melt fat, add flour, then blend in the stock and milk. Cook until thickened

6. Peel bananas, slice lengthways, then sprinkle generously with lemon juice

ROAST CHICKEN

Although traditionally served for Sunday lunch, roast chicken is delicious for any occasion. It's tender, moist and full of flavour. Served with home-made stuffing balls, roast potatoes and fresh vegetables, it's ideal for the whole family.

3-3½ lb/1.5 kg oven-ready free-range chicken
small bunch of fresh thyme
1 small onion, peeled and halved
1½ oz/40 g butter, softened
salt and freshly ground black pepper
4 rashers streaky bacon
celery leaves for garnish, optional
FOR THE STUFFING BALLS:
1 tbsp vegetable oil
1 large onion, peeled and finely chopped
6 oz/175 g fresh white breadcrumbs
3 tbsp freshly chopped parsley
finely grated rind of 1 lemon
1 tbsp dried thyme leaves
2 sticks celery, trimmed and finely chopped
salt and freshly ground black pepper
1 egg, size 3, beaten
FOR THE GRAVY:
1 oz/25 g plain flour
¾ pint/450 ml chicken stock
gravy browning, optional

Preheat oven to Gas 5, 375°F, 190°C, 10 mins before roasting the chicken. Thoroughly wash chicken, inside and outside, in cold water. Drain well and pat dry with paper towels. Place the thyme and onion halves inside the bird.

Tuck the wings and neck flap neatly under the bird. Truss the chicken neatly with thin clean string as follows: cut a length of string, about 2 ft/60 cm long. Place the centre of the string under the parson's nose, cross the ends over and tie a tight knot. Take each end over, then under the drumsticks and tie once again with a tight knot, so that the legs are held securely together. Turn the chicken over, then take the string right along the sides of the bird and under the wings to the neck end. Bring the ends across neck flap and tie securely.

Place the chicken in a roasting tin. Smear the skin with butter and season with salt and pepper. Place the bacon rashers across the breast.

Cook the chicken in the centre of the oven for 1½-1¾ hrs, or until well done, basting frequently with the pan juices. Remove the bacon rashers for the last 30 mins of cooking.

To test whether chicken is cooked, pierce the bird with the tip of a small pointed knife at the thickest part of the thigh to allow juices to run out – these should be clear with no trace of pink.

Meanwhile, make the stuffing balls.

Heat the oil in a frying pan, add the onion and cook for 5-6 mins until softened, but not browned. Place in a bowl with the remaining stuffing ingredients. Season and mix together, roll into neat balls.

About 40 mins before the chicken is cooked, take 3 tbsp of the fat from the roasting tin and put it into a shallow ovenproof dish. Add the stuffing balls, turning them in the fat until they are evenly coated. Place in the oven, on a rack above the chicken, to cook until golden brown. When the chicken is done, remove from the roasting tin and place on serving plate, loosely cover with foil and keep warm.

To make gravy, discard the bacon rashers from roasting tin. Tilt tin to one side and carefully skim off all fat from the roasting juices left in bottom of the pan. Place roasting tin on the heat and stir in the flour. Stir in the chicken stock and gravy browning if using. Bring to the boil, stirring all the time until gravy thickens. Reduce heat and simmer for 5 mins. Strain the gravy into a serving jug. Serve chicken accompanied by the stuffing balls, bacon rolls and gravy.

HANDY TIP

Try this alternative for a change. Instead of covering chicken with the bacon and smearing with butter, pour 3 tbsp clear honey mixed with 2 tbsp water over the chicken. Cover with tin foil and cook as before.

1. Truss cleaned chicken with thin string tied around parson's nose and legs

2. Turn chicken over, bring string to top of wings and tie across neck and flap

3. Place chicken in tin, smear with butter, season, place bacon across breast

4. Mix all the stuffing ingredients together, bind, and then roll into neat balls

5. For gravy, skim fat from residue left in tin and stir flour into meat juices

6. Add stock to roasting tin and bring to the boil, stirring. Cook until thickened

CHICKEN CORDON BLEU

Make tender pieces of chicken special by filling with smoked ham and delicious Gruyère cheese and coating in golden breadcrumbs. Easy when you follow this step-by-step guide.

Calories per portion: 568   **SERVES 4**

4 boneless chicken breasts, each approx 7 oz/200 g in weight
4 thin slices smoked ham
4 thin slices Gruyère cheese
salt and freshly ground black pepper
6 oz/175 g fresh white breadcrumbs
2 eggs, size 5, beaten
3 tbsp vegetable oil

Preheat the oven to Gas 5, 375°F, 190°C, 10 mins before cooking. Discard the skin from the chicken and trim off any small pieces of fat. Place the chicken breasts on a chopping board and cut along the long edge, without cutting completely in half.

Open out each chicken breast so that it lies flat. Place between two sheets of clearwrap or greaseproof paper and beat quite lightly with a meat mallet or rolling pin, until the breasts are completely flat. Don't beat too hard otherwise you'll end up with a pulp.

Arrange a thin slice of ham and then Gruyère cheese on top, trim the ham and cheese if necessary so that it fits inside the chicken breast once it has been folded over.

Season chicken breasts then fold over, returning them to their original shape. Place between two sheets of clearwrap or greaseproof paper and beat the edges lightly with the mallet or rolling pin so that they stick together. If necessary, secure the edges of the chicken breasts with cocktail sticks, but remove them before serving.

Put the stuffed chicken breasts on a plate, cover, then chill in the fridge for 30 mins. Place the breadcrumbs in the bottom of a clean grill pan then place under a preheated grill and toast lightly. Stir the breadcrumbs frequently to avoid burning them. Remove, allow to cool then place in a bowl.

Pour the beaten egg in a bowl large enough so that the chicken can easily be placed inside. Remove chicken from the fridge then dip each chicken breast in the beaten egg until thoroughly coated. Let any excess egg drip off into the bowl. Carefully roll the chicken breasts in the toasted breadcrumbs until they are evenly coated.

Place in a baking tin and drizzle the oil over. Cook in the oven for 20-30 mins or until the chicken is thoroughly cooked. (The time will vary slightly according to the weight of the chicken.) Serve immediately.

HANDY TIPS

If preferred, you can substitute brown bread instead of the white for the breadcrumbs. You can also fry the chicken breasts instead of cooking them in the oven. To fry, heat 4 tbsp oil and 2 tbsp butter together in a large frying pan. Then fry for 10 mins on each side or until cooked and the coating is crisp and golden. Drain on absorbent kitchen paper and serve immediately.

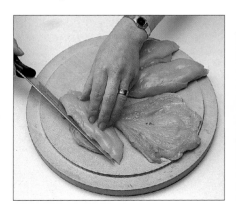

1. Place chicken on a chopping board and cut along the long edge, open out

2. Place individual breasts between sheets of clearwrap and beat lightly

3. Open chicken breasts and place slice of ham and cheese on top, fold over

4. Replace chicken breasts between clearwrap and lightly beat the edges

5. Dip stuffed chicken breasts into beaten egg until coated, drain off excess

6. Coat chicken breasts in breadcrumbs, ensuring they are completely covered

CHICKEN MARENGO

Tender succulent chicken, gently cooked in brandy and white wine, with a subtle hint of lemon. It's said that this dish was a favourite of Napoleon's and we're sure it will be a real hit with you, too.

Calories per portion: 619

SERVES 4

3½ lb/1.5 kg oven-ready
   free-range chicken

1 lemon

2 medium onions

3 oz/75 g butter or margarine

2 tbsp oil

3 tbsp French brandy

salt and freshly ground
   black pepper

¼ pint/150 ml medium dry
   white wine

½ pint/300 ml chicken stock

4 oz/100 g baby mushrooms,
   wiped

1 oz/25 g plain flour

3 tbsp single cream or
   crème fraîche

zested lemon rind and chopped
   parsley to garnish

Preheat oven to Gas 4, 350°F, 180°C, 10 mins before cooking chicken. Remove any giblets from the inside of the chicken, wash well and use to make chicken stock. Discard any fat from inside the cavity then place the chicken on a chopping board.

With a sharp kitchen knife carefully cut down along the side of the breastbone. Pull the two halves open then, using a meat cleaver, chop through the carcass to form two

HANDY TIPS

If watching your fat intake, use skinned chicken and olive oil instead of butter or margarine and fromage frais, not cream.

separate halves. (If you don't have a meat cleaver, use your kitchen knife and tap the top edge with a rolling pin to ensure a clean cut.)

Turn the halves over and cut off the scaly part of the leg. Pull the leg joint out and make a diagonal cut across to form 2 joints. Wash thoroughly under cold water and dry on absorbent paper. Cut the lemon in half and rub over the joints.

Peel and finely slice the onions. melt 1 oz/25 g of the fat with the oil in a frying pan, and fry the chicken on all sides until golden brown. Drain on absorbent paper. Place in a 4 pint/ 2.25 litre ovenproof casserole.

Fry the onions in the fat remaining in the pan for 5 mins, or until translucent. Remove from the heat, pour in brandy, add seasoning. Return to heat and cook for 1 min, then add white wine and stock. Pour over chicken then cook in oven for 1 hr or until the chicken is tender.

Meanwhile, 15 mins before end of cooking time, melt 1 oz/25 g of the remaining fat in a small saucepan. Cook mushrooms for 5 mins, drain and add to casserole. When the chicken is cooked, drain and skim, reserving stock. Place the reserved stock into a small pan and bring to the boil. Beat the remaining fat with the flour then drop small spoonfuls into the boiling stock, whisking vigorously. Cook for 2 mins or until thickened. Stir in the cream or crème fraîche, pour over chicken. Sprinkle with lemon rind and parsley.

1. With a very sharp knife, cut down along the side of the chicken breastbone

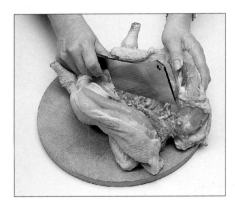

2. Pull the chicken open and, using a meat cleaver, chop completely in half

3. Take one half of the chicken, pull the leg joint out and cut in half

4. Rub the washed and dried chicken pieces all over with the cut lemon

5. Fry the chicken pieces on both sides until they are golden brown all over

6. Gently fry the onions until they are translucent, then pour in the brandy

CHICKEN CHASSEUR

Succulent chicken joints, simmered in a white wine sauce with shallots, mushrooms and just a hint of tomato. It's easy to prepare and cook and is ideal for any occasion.

Calories per portion: 595   SERVES 4

4 chicken joints
2 tbsp vegetable oil
3½ oz/90 g butter or margarine
6 oz/175 g shallots or baby onions
4 oz/100 g mushrooms
½ pint/300 ml chicken stock
½ pint/300 ml white wine
1 tbsp tomato purée
1 oz/25 g plain flour
2 tbsp freshly chopped parsley
salt and freshly ground
    black pepper
2 bay leaves

HANDY TIPS

To freeze, prepare as above but omit thickening the sauce with the butter and flour paste. Once chicken is cooked, leave until cold, then place in a freezable container and freeze.

To serve, remove from freezer and allow the chicken to thaw, preferably overnight in the bottom of the fridge. Place in casserole, heat through at Gas 4, 350°F, 180°C, for 40-50 mins. Carefully stir in the butter and flour paste halfway through re-heating.

Preheat oven to Gas 4, 350°F, 180°C, 10 mins before cooking casserole. Wipe chicken joints with a clean damp cloth, discarding any fat. Trim away any extra pieces of skin. Heat the 2 tbsp of oil and 1½ oz/40 g of the butter or margarine in pan. Fry the chicken joints until golden brown all over. Drain well on absorbent paper then place in a 4 pint/2.25 litre oven-proof casserole.

Peel shallots or baby onions, removing the root, then fry in the fat remaining in frying pan until golden. Drain and place on top of chicken. Wipe mushrooms and slice thinly, add to fat remaining in pan and cook, stirring occasionally for 3-4 mins. Drain then place on top of chicken joints and the shallots or baby onions.

Gradually pour the stock into the frying pan, stirring throughout to remove any pieces of sediment left in the pan. Stir in the wine and the tomato purée and bring to the boil. Beat the remaining 2 oz/50 g butter or margarine with the flour, then whisk in small teaspoonfuls to the boiling liquid. Whisk until smooth and thickened. Stir in the parsley, and season to taste with the salt and black pepper.

Pour the sauce over the chicken joints. Place 2 bay leaves in the sauce. Cover casserole with the lid and cook on the centre shelf for 1½-1¾ hrs or until the chicken is tender. Discard bay leaves. Check seasoning then serve sprinkled with a little extra chopped parsley and vegetables, baked potatoes, rice or tagliatelle.

1. Fry chicken joints in the oil and 1½ oz/ 40 g of the fat until golden brown all over

2. Add the shallots or baby onions to the pan and gently fry until golden

3. Slice the mushrooms thinly then fry in the pan for 3-4 mins or until lightly brown

4. Whisk in small spoonfuls of the butter and flour paste

5. Stir in the chopped parsley to the thickened sauce

6. Pour the sauce over the chicken, cover casserole with a lid and cook

PEKING DUCK

With its crisp, tangy skin, Peking Duck is the most popular of all Chinese dishes. Serve with cool cucumber, spring onion strips and a rich plum Hoisin sauce. Wrapped in featherlight pancakes, it's delicious.

Calories per portion: 964 **SERVES 6**

5 lb/2.25 kg oven-ready duck
4 tbsp Chinese five spice powder
2 tsp salt
4 tbsp clear honey
1 tbsp white wine vinegar
1 tbsp medium dry sherry
3 tbsp light soy sauce
FOR THE PANCAKES:
8 oz/225 g strong plain flour
1 tbsp sesame oil
TO SERVE:
1 bunch spring onions
½ small cucumber
Hoisin sauce

Preheat oven to Gas 6, 400°F, 200°C, 15 mins before cooking duck.

If the duck is frozen, ensure it is thoroughly thawed before use. Rinse and pat dry with absorbent paper. Mix the Chinese five spice powder with the 2 tsp salt and sprinkle inside the duck cavity. Pinch the duck all over with the forefinger and thumb to help break down the fat and to loosen the skin from the bird.

Place the duck in a roasting tin or a large ovenproof bowl and scald by pouring boiling water over. Drain and allow to dry in a cool, airy place for at least 2-3 hrs. The longer you leave the duck to dry the crisper the skin will be.

HANDY TIP

Make the pancakes in advance, then freeze until required. Thaw before using. Reheat as above, in a steamer.

The Chinese hang them up to dry overnight before cooking.

Mix the honey, wine vinegar, sherry and soy sauce with ¼ pint/150 ml boiling water and stir until thoroughly blended. Put duck on a trivet in a roasting tin. Pour marinade over and roast for 1½-2 hrs. To test if cooked, the juices should run clear when the leg is pierced with a skewer.

Meanwhile make the pancakes: mix the flour with 6 fl oz/175 ml hot water to form a dough, knead until smooth then leave to relax for 30 mins. Cover with clean cloth. Divide dough into small pieces then roll out to 2 in/5 cm rounds. Brush one side with sesame oil and place two pancakes together, oiled sides innermost. Roll out again until the pancakes are really thin, cut each into 7 in/18 cm rounds. Heat a non-stick frying pan over a gentle heat. Fry pancakes until dry on one side, turn over and cook the other side. Repeat until all the pancakes are cooked. When it's time to eat, reheat in a steamer over gently boiling water.

Trim spring onions to 3 in/7.5 cm lengths. Take half and using a sharp knife, make very thin cuts to 1 in/2.5 cm of base. Place in a bowl of iced water for 2-3 hrs: this will make the ends curl decoratively. Shred remainder. Peel cucumber, cut into ¼ in/6 mm thin strips. To eat, shred or carve the duck. Spread a spoonful of sauce on to pancakes. Top with shredded spring onions and strips of cucumber and duck. Roll up filled pancakes to eat.

1. *Pinch the duck all over with thumb and forefinger to break down the fat*

2. *Place seasoned duck in a large roasting tin, pour boiling water over, drain*

3. *Put the duck on a trivet, mix the marinade then pour over and roast*

4. To make the pancakes: add water to the sifted flour and bind to a stiff dough

5. Knead dough on a floured board then roll out small pieces to 2 in/5 cm rounds

6. Trim cleaned spring onions to 3 in/ 7.5 cm. Make cuts 1 in/2.5 cm from base

ROAST BEEF

It's great at any time of the year! Served traditionally with roast potatoes, sprouts and horseradish sauce, a roast is equally delicious with new potatoes, baby carrots and fresh peas. Try it cold next day with bubble and squeak.

Calories per portion: 760   **SERVES 8**

**I piece wing rib, 2 or 3 ribs
    approx 3-5 lb/1.5-2.25 kg
    in weight**
**I oz/25 g lard or white
    vegetable fat**
salt
FOR THE YORKSHIRE PUDDING:
4 oz/100 g plain flour
2 eggs, size 3
**½ pint/300 ml milk or milk and
    water mixed**
**I oz/25 g lard or white vegetable
    fat or 1½ tbsp fat from
    roasting meat**
FOR THE GRAVY:
3 tbsp fat from roasting meat
1½ -2 tbsp plain flour
**½ pint/300 ml beef or vegetable
    stock – you can use some of
    the vegetable cooking water**
½ -1 tsp gravy browning, optional

Preheat oven to Gas 7, 425°F, 220°C, 15 mins before roasting the beef. Weigh the joint and calculate the cooking time, allowing 20 mins per lb plus 20 mins-slightly less if rare meat is required. Cut away the bone at base of joint, but leave in place to ensure easy carving. Wipe the meat with a clean, damp cloth. Tie round the joint with string in two or three places and put in a large roasting tin, ensuring that the cut sides are exposed to the heat and the thickest area of fat is uppermost. This way, the fat keeps the meat moist during cooking.

Dot with small knobs of fat and season with salt. Roast in centre of oven for calculated length of cooking time. Towards the end of cooking time pour off 1½ tbsp fat, if using, for Yorkshire Pudding and 3 tbsp of fat for gravy.

To make Yorkshire Pudding, sift flour into mixing bowl, make a well in centre,

drop in eggs. Gradually beat in milk, bringing in the flour from the sides of the bowl. Beat to a smooth batter. Heat lard or fat either in a small roasting tin 8 in x 6 in/20 cm x 15 cm or in individual patty tins until smoking. Pour in batter and return to oven, towards the top. Cook large pudding for 30-40 mins or individual puddings for 15-20 mins, or until well risen.

To make the gravy, heat fat from meat in a small saucepan, stir in flour and cook for 2 mins. Remove from

heat and stir in stock, gravy browning, if using, and any of the meat juices left in the roasting tin, and seasoning to taste. Return gravy to heat and cook, stirring throughout, until smooth and thickened.

HANDY TIP

Using two eggs in your Yorkshire Pudding and ensuring that the fat is really hot and the oven temperature is correct, produces perfect results every time.

1. Cut the bone away from base of meat but leave in position for easy carving

2. Tie joint in two or three places to keep meat a good shape during cooking

3. Place in a roasting tin. Dot with small pieces of fat and season with salt.

4. Make a well in centre of flour, drop in eggs then beat to a batter with milk.

5. Heat a little fat in the patty tins and then when smoking, pour in batter

6. Heat fat from roasting tin, stir in flour, cook for 2 mins, then slowly add stock

STEAK & STOUT PIE

Make a perfect pie of tender pieces of steak, carrots, mushrooms and tomatoes, simmered in stout, then topped with mouthwatering, crisp shortcrust pastry. Serve it with fresh vegetables to warm them up deliciously when it's cold outside.

Calories per portion: 581   **SERVES 4**

1 lb/450 g braising steak, trimmed
2 small onions
2 carrots
2 large tomatoes
2 tbsp oil
2 tsp sugar
2 bay leaves
salt and freshly ground
    black pepper
2 tbsp flour
½ pint/300 ml stout
½ pint/300 ml beef stock
4 oz/100 g button mushrooms
8 oz/225 g prepared shortcrust
    pastry, thawed if frozen
beaten egg or milk to glaze

Preheat the oven to Gas 6, 400°F, 200°C, 15 mins before baking. Cut the beef into 1 in/2.5 cm cubes. Peel and thinly slice the onions and carrots. Make a small cross in the top of each tomato, then cover with boiling water and leave for 2 mins. Drain. Peel the tomatoes,

discard seeds, then roughly chop the flesh and reserve.

Heat the oil in a large saucepan, then fry meat in small batches, stirring, until browned. Remove each batch with a draining spoon and reserve. When all the meat has been browned, add the onions and carrots to the pan, then cook gently for 5 mins, or until softened. Return the meat to the pan, then add the chopped tomatoes, sugar and bay leaves. Season. Sprinkle with the flour and continue cooking over a very gentle heat for 2 mins. Gradually stir in the stout and beef stock, bring to the boil, then cover and gently simmer for 1½ hrs, stirring occasionally.

Wipe the mushrooms, then add to the pan and continue to cook for a further 10 mins. Leave to cool. Using approx 1½ oz/40 g shortcrust pastry, roll out, on a lightly floured surface, a thin strip wide enough to fix to the edge of a 2½ pint/1.5 litre pie dish.

HANDY TIP

If preferred cook the meat in the oven at Gas 4, 350°F, 180°C, for 2 hrs, then add mushrooms and allow to cool before proceeding with the pie.

Spoon cooled filling into the pie dish, then roll out remaining pastry and cut out a lid, large enough to cover top of dish completely. Dampen pastry strip, then wrap the pastry lid round the rolling pin and place on top of pie. Pinch the edges securely together and make a decorative border around the edge. Use any pastry trimmings to decorate the top of the pie, then brush with the beaten egg or milk.

Bake in the oven for 15 mins, then brush again with the egg or milk and continue to cook for a further 15 mins, or until the pastry is golden brown. Serve hot with cooked vegetables.

1. Cut meat into 1 in/2.5 cm cubes, then peel and slice the onions and carrots

2. Fry the meat in small batches until browned, then drain and reserve

3. Return meat to pan, add tomatoes, sugar, bay leaves, seasoning and flour

4. Place a spoonful of stuffing in centre of the pastry, then top with steak

5. Dampen edges of pastry, then bring edges up and over to encase steak

6. Roll out the pastry trimmings, then cut out strips and decorate the parcels

BEEF CARBONNADE

There's nothing more appetizing than the smell of Beef Carbonnade as it cooks. Tender strips of beef, thinly sliced onions and a hint of garlic simmered in a delicious rich sauce.

Calories per portion: 606   **SERVES 4**

1½ lb/675 g braising steak

2 large onions

2 garlic cloves, optional

3 oz/75 g butter or margarine

1½ oz/40 g flour

¾ pint/450 ml light ale

¼ pint/150 ml beef stock

1 tbsp tarragon vinegar

2 tsp sugar

2 bay leaves

salt and freshly ground
    black pepper

1 tbsp freshly chopped parsley

HANDY TIP

You can make your own speciality herb vinegars quite easily. Place a sprig or two of the herb of your choice in a screw-top bottle. Fill up with either a white vinegar or wine vinegar. Leave for a couple of months before using.

Preheat oven to Gas 4, 350°F, 180°C, 10 mins before cooking carbonnade.

Discard any fat or gristle from steak, then cut into strips 3 in/7.5 cm long x 1 in/2.5 cm wide. Remember when slicing beef – to help ensure the meat will be tender, slice across the grain. Peel onions and slice thinly. Peel and crush garlic, if using. Melt butter or margarine in frying pan, then cook the onions and garlic for 5 mins or until soft and transparent. Drain and place in an oven-proof casserole.

Fry the meat in the fat left in the pan, stirring with a wooden spoon until the meat is browned completely. Drain and place on top of onions. Sprinkle the flour into pan and cook, stirring carefully throughout until all the flour is incorporated into the juices left in the pan. Cook for a further 1 min and gradually stir in the light ale, then the stock. Bring to the boil and continue to cook until mixture thickens.

Stir in the vinegar, sugar, bay leaves, salt and freshly ground black pepper to taste. Cook for a further 2 mins. Pour over the meat and onions and mix well together.

Cover with a lid and cook in oven for 2-2½ hrs or until meat is tender – stir the carbonnade occasionally during cooking. Discard bay leaves, check seasoning and sprinkle with parsley.

In France this dish is served with plenty of bread so the rich, tasty gravy can be soaked up and none of it is wasted. Or serve with mashed or baked potatoes.

1. Trim beef, discard fat and gristle, cut into 3 in x 1 in//7.5 cm x 2.5 cm strips

2. Thinly slice the peeled onions. It's easier if you leave the root on when slicing

3. Melt the butter or margarine and fry onions until soft and transparent

4. Fry meat in fat remaining in pan until browned. Stir with a wooden spoon

5. Gradually add ale to the pan, stirring throughout to prevent lumps

6. Mix in the vinegar, sugar, salt and ground black pepper and bay leaves

BOILED BEEF & CARROTS

This delicious dish is an old English classic. Tender beef, simmered gently with carrots, onions, celery and spices, is served with light fluffy dumplings. A warming and mouth-watering meal for cold, wintry evenings.

Calories per portion: 732

SERVES 6

3 lb/1.5 kg salted rolled brisket

1 tbsp oil

2 carrots

1 large or 2 medium onions

2 sticks celery

2 bay leaves

a few cloves

a few black peppercorns

FOR THE DUMPLINGS:

4 oz/100 g self-raising flour

2 oz/50 g shredded vegetable suet

1 tsp dried mustard

1 tbsp freshly chopped parsley
   or 1 tsp dried parsley

salt and freshly ground
   black pepper

If necessary, soak the brisket to remove any excess salt (ask your butcher how long it needs), then tie the joint securely in 3-4 places to ensure it keeps its shape during cooking. Heat oil in a frying pan, then brown joint on all sides to seal in the juices. Place in a large flameproof casserole suitable for cooking on top of the hob. Alternatively, use a large saucepan. Cover the joint completely with cold water, bring to the boil, then skim off the surface scum.

Peel carrots and cut in half if large. Peel and cut the onions into chunks. Scrub celery and cut into chunks. Add vegetables to pan with bay leaves, cloves and peppercorns. Reduce heat, cover, then simmer gently for about 1½ hrs. Remove two thirds of the vegetables, the meat (and the remaining vegetables) should continue cooking for a further 30 mins or so.

Meanwhile make the dumplings: sieve flour into a mixing bowl. Stir in shredded vegetable suet, mustard, parsley and seasoning. Make a well in the centre, gradually stir in approx 6-7 tbsp cold water and mix to form a soft, pliable (but not sticky) mixture. Dampen hands with cold water, then shape mixture into balls the size of walnuts. Drop dumplings into casserole liquid 15 mins before end of meat cooking time.

Return the reserved vegetables to the casserole, heat through. Serve with the beef and dumplings, along with freshly cooked cabbage and a little of the cooking liquid.

If preferred, serve with parsley sauce: melt 1 oz/25 g fat in a pan, stir in 1 oz/25 g flour and cook for 1 min. Remove from heat and gradually blend in ¼ pint/150 ml cooking liquid and ¾ pint/450 ml milk. Stir in 3 tbsp chopped parsley and bring to the boil, stirring.

Season and serve.

HANDY TIP

Salted topside or silverside can be used instead of salted rolled brisket.

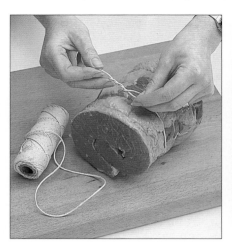

1. Tie the joint in 3-4 places to ensure it keeps its shape during cooking

2. Heat the oil in a pan, then brown the joint on all sides to seal in the juices

3. Place joint in casserole, cover with water, bring to the boil, then skim

4. Add the carrots, chopped onion, celery, bay leaves and spices to casserole

5. Place flour, suet, mustard, parsley and seasoning in a bowl. Mix with water

6. Shape dumplings to the size of walnuts and then drop into the casserole

STEAK PUDDINGS

Tender chunks of steak flavoured with onions and mushrooms, encased in a suet pastry, this delicious dish is a traditional family favourite. Just follow this easy step-by-step recipe for a hearty meal that everyone is sure to love.

6 oz/175 g self-raising flour
3 oz/75 g shredded vegetable suet
pinch of salt
FOR THE FILLING:
1 small onion
4 oz/100 g braising steak
2 oz/50 g mushrooms
1 level tbsp freshly
    chopped parsley
salt and freshly ground
    black pepper
1 tsp flour
2-3 tbsp beef stock, optional

Lightly grease four individual steamed pudding or dariole moulds. If liked, you can cut out four small rounds of greaseproof paper to fit the base of each mould (this will help when turning out the puddings).

Place the self-raising flour in a bowl, add suet and salt, mix to a soft, pliable dough with approx 9 tbsp cold water. Knead until smooth but not sticky. Roll out dough on a lightly floured surface and cut out four 4 in/10 cm rounds. Fold each round in half, then into quarters. Place inside moulds, then carefully ease the pastry into the base and up the sides, ensuring there are no

HANDY TIP

The filling can be varied according to personal preference. Try using 1½ tsp dried mixed herbs in place of the parsley, or add 1 finely chopped or crushed garlic clove to the mixture.

air bubbles or cracks. Roll the remaining pastry together, cut out four lids and reserve.

To make the filling, peel, then finely chop the onion and place in a bowl. Trim braising steak then cut into ¼ in/6 mm cubes. Add to the onion. Wipe the mushrooms, chop finely, then add to onion and meat with the parsley and seasoning to taste. Sprinkle the flour over and toss all the ingredients together. Moisten with 2-3 tbsp beef stock, if using, or cold water.

Spoon the filling into the pastry-lined moulds, packing it down firmly. Dampen the edges of the pastry with water, then place the lids in position and pinch the edges firmly together. Cover each mould with pleated greaseproof paper and pudding cloth or foil, securing firmly with string.

Place puddings in the top of a steamer over a pan of gently boiling water. Steam steadily for 2 hrs, replenishing water as necessary.

Remove puddings from steamer and allow to stand for 3-5 mins. Using a round-bladed knife, carefully loosen around edges, then invert puddings on to a warm serving plate. Serve immediately with freshly cooked vegetables and gravy.

1. Roll dough on a lightly floured surface, cut out four rounds and fold into quarters

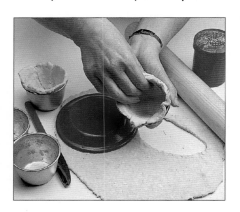

2. Place each round into lightly greased mould, easing it into base and sides

3. Finely chop onion, place in bowl. Trim steak cut into cubes, then add to onion

4. Finely chop mushrooms, add to the bowl, with chopped parsley and seasoning

5. Spoon the prepared filling into pastry-lined moulds, packing it down firmly

6. Dampen edges of pastry with water, place lids in position and seal firmly

SHEPHERD'S PIE

This popular family dish is a simple and tasty way of using up cold leftover lamb. It can be served with a mixed salad or your favourite freshly cooked vegetables – either way it's just the thing for a delicious lunch or a supper treat.

Calories per portion: 427   **SERVES 6**

2 lb/900 g potatoes, peeled
1 lb/450 g leftover roast lamb
1 large onion
2 large carrots
2 tbsp olive oil
1 oz/25 g plain flour
1 tbsp dried mixed herbs
1 tbsp tomato purée
14 oz/397 g can tomatoes, drained and chopped
½ pint/300 ml lamb stock or leftover lamb gravy
salt and freshly ground black pepper
2 oz/50g butter
2-3 tbsp milk

Preheat oven to Gas 7, 425°F, 220°C, 15 mins before cooking the Shepherd's Pie. Cut the potatoes into small pieces, cook in boiling, salted water for 15 mins, until soft.

Meanwhile, cut the cooked lamb off the bone then cut into small pieces, discarding any fat or gristle, then chop with a large knife. (To make the job quicker, use two evenly weighted knives, holding one in each hand. Chop the meat by letting the knives fall alternately and rhythmically.) Alternatively if you have a mincer, pass the meat through using the coarse cutter.

Peel the onion, then chop finely. Peel carrots, trim, then cut into small cubes. Heat the oil in a large frying pan, add the onion and carrot and cook over a low heat for 10-15 mins until softened but not browned. Stir in the flour and herbs, cook for 2 mins, then add tomato purée, tomatoes, chopped lamb and the stock or gravy. Bring to the boil, stirring all the time. Allow to simmer for 5 mins. Season well with salt and pepper. Remove from the heat and spoon into an ovenproof dish, smooth the top and set aside.

Drain the cooked potatoes, mash well, then add 1 oz/25 g butter, milk and seasoning to taste. Beat until smooth and creamy, then spread mashed potatoes evenly over the lamb. Mark the top with a criss-cross pattern using a fork or palette knife.

Melt remaining butter in a small pan then brush melted butter carefully over the potato. Cook in oven for 35-40 mins until golden brown and thoroughly heated through.

Serve with baked tomatoes and spring greens.

HANDY TIPS

Shepherd's Pie freezes really well. You can prepare the pie, but omit brushing the top with the melted butter. Allow pie to cool, then cover and label before freezing.

To cook – allow to thaw in the fridge overnight, then brush top with the butter and cook as before. If preferred, the onion and carrots can be minced coarsely as well.

1. Cut the cooked lamb off the bone in thick slices, discarding any gristle

2. Cut slices into small pieces, then chop using one or two large knives

3. Fry onion and carrots in the oil until they are softened, but not browned

4. Add the flour and mixed herbs and cook for 2 mins, stirring throughout

5. Add lamb, tomato purée, tomatoes and stock. Bring to boil, simmer 5 mins

6. Spoon lamb into an ovenproof dish, then cover with the mashed potatoes

BEEF TOURNEDOS

Delicious, tender steaks that just melt in the mouth – served on croûtons of fried bread with pâté and topped with a pat of maître d'hôtel beurre. With a rich red wine sauce, perfect for a special occasion.

FOR THE MAÎTRE D'HÔTEL BEURRE:

4 oz/100 g unsalted butter

2 tbsp freshly chopped parsley

freshly ground black pepper

2-3 tbsp lemon juice

FOR THE MAIN DISH:

3 oz/75 g mushrooms

6 slices white bread

6 tournedos (fillet steak), each about 6oz/175g in weight

salt and freshly ground black pepper

2½ oz/65 g unsalted butter

2 tbsp vegetable oil

1 tbsp plain flour

8 fl oz/250 ml Madeira or red wine

6 slices smooth pâté (about 6 oz/175 g total weight)

4 tbsp double cream

Beat together all the ingredients for the maître d'hôtel beurre until well mixed. Form into a long roll about 1½ in/4 cm thick. Wrap in greaseproof paper and chill until required.

HANDY TIPS

Tournedos are small round slices of beef normally 1½ in/4 cm thick, taken from the middle of a fillet of beef. The classic tournedos recipe is served with pâté de foie gras and slices of truffle. Other names for this cut include filet mignon and châteaubriand, the latter is usually served whole.

Wipe or wash and dry mushrooms and slice thinly. Leave to one side. Cut out six 4 in/10 cm rounds from bread and leave on one side.

Lightly wash and dry the steaks, discarding any fat and trim to a neat round. Season on both sides with salt and pepper. Melt 1 oz/25 g of the butter with the oil in a frying pan then cook the steaks on both sides over a moderate heat. Cook for 2-3 mins on each side for rare, 4-5 mins each side for medium and 6-8 mins both sides for well done. When cooked, remove from pan, draining well, and keep hot.

Melt ½ oz/15 g of the remaining butter in a separate pan, add mushrooms and cook for 2 mins. Pour off all but about 1 tbsp of the butter left in pan then sprinkle in the flour. Cook, stirring for 2 mins, then gradually stir in the madeira or wine, allow to simmer for 5 mins.

Meanwhile melt the remaining 1 oz/25 g butter in the cleaned frying pan then fry the rounds of bread on both sides for 1-2 mins or until golden brown and crisp. Drain well on absorbent paper.

Cut six 4 in/10 cm rounds from the pâté then place on top of fried bread. Top with the steaks and place a knob of maître d'hôtel beurre on top. Place on a warmed serving dish.

Pour the double cream into the wine sauce and mix well. Heat through then pour around the tournedos. Serve any extra sauce separately. Serve immediately with vegetables of your choice.

1. Form butter into 1½ in/4 cm thick roll. Wrap in greaseproof paper

2. Trim steak with a sharp knife, discard any fat and shape into neat rounds

3. Heat butter and oil in pan. Fry steaks on both sides. Drain and keep hot

4. Cook mushrooms in remaining butter for 2 mins then slowly add the wine

5. Fry bread in cleaned pan for 2-3 mins each side, until crisp and golden

6. When ingredients are cooked, assemble tournedos, place on serving dish

CHILLI CON CARNE

This famous Mexican dish can be as fiery or as mild as you like, depending on how brave you're feeling! Made with lean minced beef, tomatoes, red kidney beans and chillies, it's an economical meal that's always popular.

Calories per portion: 440   **SERVES 4**

2-3 fresh chillies
1 lb/450 g ripe tomatoes
1-2 garlic cloves
1 large onion
1 tbsp oil
1 lb/450 g lean minced beef
1 tbsp flour
salt and freshly ground
     black pepper
2 tbsp tomato purée
¼ pint/150 ml beef stock
15 oz/432 g can red kidney beans
fresh coriander sprigs

HANDY TIPS

Dried chillies or chilli powder can be substituted for the fresh chillies. Use 1-2 tsp, depending on how fiery you like your food. You can also buy dried red kidney beans. If using these, soak overnight in cold water. Next day, drain, place in pan, cover with cold water. Bring to the boil and boil vigorously for 10 mins. Reduce heat, cover and simmer for 30 mins, drain. Add to the frying pan with the other chilli ingredients and cook for 15 mins.

Cut the tops from the fresh chillies, scoop out and discard the seeds. Wash thoroughly under cold water. (Wash your hands really well after handling fresh chillies and never touch your eyes, mouth or nose while preparing them as the seeds burn when in contact with the skin.)

Make a small cross in the top of each tomato, place in a large bowl and cover with boiling water. Leave for 2 mins, then drain. Peel and discard the skins. Cut tomatoes into quarters, scoop out and discard seeds, then chop roughly.

Peel the garlic cloves, then peel and finely chop the onion. Crush the chillies and garlic cloves in a pestle and mortar. Alternatively, chop finely, either in a food processor or on a board with a sharp knife.

Heat the oil, then fry the chopped onion with the garlic and chillies for 5 mins, or until the onion is soft and transparent. Add the minced beef and continue to fry, stirring frequently with a wooden spoon, until the beef is browned all over. Ensure the meat is well broken up and not in large lumps. Add the chopped tomatoes, then sprinkle in the flour, with salt and pepper to taste. Cook for 1 min, then stir in the tomato purée and stock. Bring to the boil, then cover and simmer for 30 mins.

Drain kidney beans and rinse under cold water, add to pan and continue to cook for a further 15 mins. Serve hot with freshly cooked long grain rice, garnished with fresh coriander.

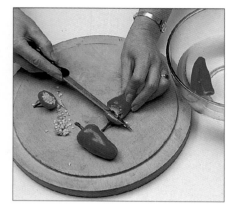

1. Cut tops off chillies and scoop out seeds. Rinse well, then wash your hands

2. Put tomatoes in boiling water for 2 mins, peel, quarter and discard seeds

3. Crush chillies and garlic in a pestle and mortar or chop in a processor

4. Fry the chopped onion in oil for 5 mins with crushed chillies and garlic

5. Fry the minced beef in frying pan, stirring throughout, until browned

6. When beef is browned, add the chopped tomatoes and seasoning

BEEF STROGANOFF

Succulent strips of beef make a mouth-watering combination with tangy onions and lightly cooked mushrooms in a rich creamy sauce. Perfect for when you want to impress on that extra special occasion.

Calories per portion: 628

SERVES 4

1½ lb/675 g fillet steak

1 oz/25 g plain flour

salt and freshly ground
    black pepper

3 large onions

3 oz/75 g butter or margarine

4 oz/100 g button mushrooms

½ pint/300 ml beef stock

2 tbsp tomato purée

½ tsp freshly grated nutmeg

¼ pint/150 ml soured cream

Trim the steak, discarding any fat or gristle. Cut the steak into thin strips ½ in/1.25 cm wide × 3 in/7.5 cm long. Place the flour on a large plate and season well with salt and pepper. Use to coat the steak.

Peel the onions and slice thinly. Then melt 1½ oz/40 g of the fat in a large heavy-based saucepan and fry the onions for 5 mins until softened but not browned. Remove from the pan

and reserve.

Add the remaining fat to the pan, then fry the steak a little at a time until browned all over. Drain on absorbent paper. Wash and dry the mushrooms and, if liked, cut in half. Fry in the remaining fat left in the pan. Drain.

Pour off any excess fat from pan then return onions, steak and mushrooms and any flour left from coating the steak. Cook gently for

2 mins, gradually stirring in the stock, then add the tomato purée. Mix well, bring to the boil, then reduce heat and allow to simmer gently for 8-10 mins or until steak is tender. Adjust seasoning if necessary and add the nutmeg. Stir in the soured cream and heat through for a further 3 mins or until piping hot. Do not allow the Stroganoff to boil at this point, otherwise the cream will curdle.

Serve with freshly cooked new potatoes which have been lightly tossed in a little butter and a crisp salad of your choice .

HANDY TIPS

If you don't want to use fillet steak you can use any other frying or grilling steak, such as rump or sirloin. You will have to increase the cooking time slightly but it will not spoil the flavour. For an even cheaper version, buy blade steak. Ensure you discard the thick piece of gristle that runs through the centre of this cut of meat. Cut the meat into really thin strips. Cook for at least 40-50 mins or until tender, stirring occasionally to prevent the Stroganoff sticking to the base of the pan and add a little extra stock if necessary. And for a change, substitute the steak for pork tenderloin and cook as above. If you're weight watching, just substitute the soured cream for fromage frais. NB: Nutmeg comes from Indonesia and the flavour is far stronger if bought whole and freshly grated just before use.

1. Trim the steak, discarding any fat and gristle and cut into thin strips, ½ in/ 1.25 cm wide x 3 in/7.5 cm in length

2. Season the flour with salt and ground black pepper. Toss the beef strips in the seasoned flour until completely coated

3. Melt 1½ oz/40 g of the butter or margarine in a heavy-based pan. Fry the onions for 5 mins. Remove from pan

4. Add remaining butter or margarine to pan, fry steak a little at a time until browned all over. Drain on absorbent

5. Return onions, beef and mushrooms to the pan with any remaining flour, then stir in the stock, then tomato purée

6. Adjust seasoning and add grated nutmeg. Stir in the soured cream and heat through for 3 mins or until piping hot

ROAST LAMB

This mouthwatering dish of succulent, tender slices of roast lamb, delicately flavoured with garlic and rosemary, is an ideal choice for a traditional Sunday roast. What makes this dish truly irresistible is its tangy apricot sauce.

Calories per portion: 394   **SERVES 6**

I leg of lamb, preferably English
    or Welsh, approx 4 lb/1.75 kg
    in weight
1-2 garlic cloves
sprigs of fresh rosemary
salt and freshly ground
    black pepper
2 tbsp olive oil
FOR THE APRICOT SAUCE:
14 oz/397g can apricots in
    natural juice
1 cinnamon stick
1 oz/25g butter
3 tbsp wine vinegar
1 oz/25g demerara sugar
1 tsp freshly grated nutmeg

Preheat oven to Gas 8, 450°F, 230°C, 15 mins before roasting lamb. Wipe the lamb with a clean damp cloth and then place on a clean surface. Cut off the shank bone just above the knuckle. Turn the joint round and cut the exposed surface round the pelvic bone. Cut deep into the flesh, following the shape of the bone. When you have exposed the ball and socket joint, sever the tendons joining the pelvic bone to the thigh bone. Remove pelvic bone. Cut away any excess fat.

Peel the garlic cloves, then cut into thin slivers. Using a sharp knife, make small incisions just under the skin and insert the slivers of garlic. This will ensure that, during cooking, the flavour of the garlic penetrates the whole joint of lamb. Place small sprigs of rosemary into the cuts in which you have inserted the garlic. Season with the salt and freshly ground black pepper.

Place in a roasting tin, brush with olive oil, then roast in the oven. For your cooking time, allow 10-12 mins per 1 lb/450 g plus 12 mins for pink meat, 15-20 mins per 1 lb/450 g plus 20 mins for medium lamb, 25-30 mins per 1 lb/450 g plus 25 mins for well cooked meat. After 10 mins, reduce heat to Gas 4, 350°F, 180°C, and continue to roast for the calculated cooking time. Baste the meat from time to time during cooking. When it's cooked, remove from the oven. Pour off the juice, reserving it for gravy, and allow the joint to stand for 10 mins before carving.

To make the apricot sauce, purée the contents of the can of apricots in a food processor or blender until smooth. Pour into a small saucepan. Lightly bruise the cinnamon stick, add to the pan with the butter, wine vinegar and sugar. Finely grate the nutmeg into the pan. Heat the sauce through gently, stir occasionally and allow to simmer for 8-10 mins. Discard cinnamon stick before serving.

HANDY TIPS

If preferred use 8 oz/225 g no-need-to-soak apricots to make the sauce. Simmer apricots in ¼ pint/150 ml water for 10 mins then purée.

1. Cut off the shank bone just above the knuckle and small bone at pelvic end

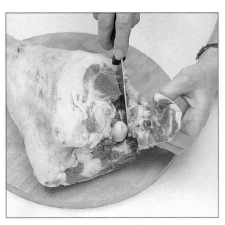

2. Remove pelvic bone, cut deep into flesh, following contours of the bone

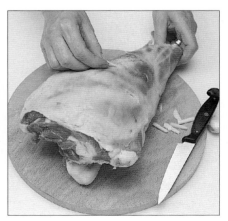

3. Cut garlic clove into slivers, then insert into lamb, just under the skin

4. Insert small sprigs of fresh rosemary into the same holes as the garlic

5. Purée apricots in a food processor or blender until smooth, pour into pan

6. Add wine vinegar, butter and sugar. Finely grate nutmeg, then add to pan

NOISETTES OF LAMB

Tender succulent cuts of lamb with a delicious creamy raspberry sauce. Perfect for a summer treat or when you want to impress. The secret is in the preparation, just follow the easy steps for a mouthwatering meal to remember.

1. Ask the butcher to saw through chine bone then cut down each side, discard

2. Cut between each rib bone and discard, leave as much meat as possible

3. After boning rack of lamb, hold meat firmly then pull the skin away

1 whole English or Welsh best
    end of neck, approx
    12-16 chops in all
salt and freshly ground
    black pepper
2 tbsp oil
2 tbsp flour
¼ pint/150 ml lamb or
    vegetable stock
12 oz/350 g raspberries
3 tbsp redcurrant jelly
¼ pint/150 ml crème fraîche
fresh mint leaves

Ask your butcher to saw through the chine bone of the lamb. Using a very sharp knife, cut down between the chine bone and the edge of the meat, then carefully remove the chine bone. Place the rack skin side down on a board, then, using a very sharp knife, carefully cut down each side of the rib bones. Ease the bone up and cut down the back of the bone, remove. Repeat this until all the bones are removed, then remove any cartilage that lies at the tip of the meat.

Turn the meat over and, holding it firmly with one hand, take the top edge of the skin and pull it away from the lamb. Don't try and cut it away as you will not get an even surface, which will affect the finished look of the noisettes. Trim away any pieces of cartilage or bone.

Cut the rack in half, season with salt and freshly ground black pepper. Place the racks, meat uppermost, then roll into neat rolls, tucking in any odd pieces of meat. Tie the meat at 2 in/5 cm intervals. Cut into four.

Brush the noisettes with a little oil. Preheat the grill, then place the noisettes on the grill rack and cook for 5-8 mins each side, depending on how

thick the noisettes are and how pink you like your lamb. Remove from the rack, place on a serving plate and keep hot.

Drain off the fat from the grill pan and place in a small pan. Hull raspberries, rinse lightly. Purée 10 oz/300 g of the raspberries in a food processor then sieve to remove pips.

Heat the reserved fat, sift in the flour and cook for 2 mins. Remove from the heat and stir in the stock, raspberry purée and add redcurrant jelly. Return to the heat and cook, stirring throughout until the sauce thickens and the jelly has melted.

Season with salt and pepper then stir in the crème fraîche. Heat through until hot but do not allow to boil. Garnish noisettes with remaining raspberries and mint leaves. Serve with prepared sauce and vegetables of your choice.

4. Cut the meat in half then neatly roll both pieces up, tuck in any spare meat

5. Tie meat with string to form a neat roll. Use a double knot to make it secure

6. Using a sharp knife, cut each roll into four 2 in/5 cm thick noisettes

ROGHAN JOSH

Tasty chunks of lamb in a rich, mild yogurt sauce, with a hint of spice. This authentic curry is perfect for entertaining friends. Serve with poppadoms, tangy lime pickle, nutty rice and a cool cucumber raita for a true taste of India.

Calories per portion: 812   **SERVES 4**

2 in/5 cm piece root ginger

10 garlic cloves, peeled

¼ pint/150 ml vegetable oil

2 lb/900 g shoulder of lamb,
    boned, trimmed and cubed

12 green cardamom pods

2 fresh bay leaves

8 cloves

12 black peppercorns

2 in/5 cm piece cinnamon stick

8 oz/225 g onions, peeled
    and chopped

1½ tsp ground coriander

2½ tsp ground cumin

5 tsp paprika

1½ tsp cayenne pepper

1½ tsp salt

3 fl oz/75 ml low-fat
    natural yogurt

½ tsp garam masala

fresh coriander sprigs to garnish

FOR THE RICE:

1 tbsp oil

12 oz/350 g basmati rice

1 oz/25 g flaked almonds

½ tsp salt

6 green cardamom pods

1 tsp turmeric

HANDY TIPS

Yogurt is added to many Indian dishes and adds a delicate creamy texture to the dish with a subtle tartness. It must be added 1 tbsp at a time and allowed to be absorbed in the sauce before the next addition, otherwise the sauce may curdle.

Peel and finely chop the root ginger. Place in food processor with garlic and 5 tbsp water. Blend to form a smooth paste. Reserve. Heat half the oil in a large frying pan. Fry meat until sealed. Remove from pan and reserve. Place the cardamom pods, bay leaves, cloves, peppercorns and cinnamon stick in frying pan with remaining oil. Cook for 1 min. Add onions and cook for 5 mins. Stir in reserved garlic and ginger paste, coriander, cumin, paprika, cayenne and salt. Cook for 1 min, stirring well to mix the spices.

Return meat to pan. Stir well. Cook for 2 mins. Add yogurt, 1 tbsp at a time, stirring well. Cook for further 5-6 mins. Add ½ pint/300 ml water, stirring. Bring to boil. Reduce heat, cover, simmer for 1 hr. If preferred the lamb can be cooked in the oven, Gas 4, 350°F, 180°C for 1 hr.

Remove lid and cook, uncovered, for 30 mins, or until the meat is tender and liquid has reduced to form a thick reddish sauce.

Meanwhile, cook the rice. Heat the oil in a frying pan. Add rice, almonds, salt and cardamom pods. Fry for 3 mins. Add turmeric and 1½ pints/900 ml water, bring to boil, then simmer for 15-20 mins until liquid is absorbed and the rice is cooked.

Remove Roghan Josh from heat, skim off any excess oil. Place in warmed serving dish. Sprinkle with garam masala, garnish with coriander sprigs. Serve with the rice and a cucumber raita.

1. Blend ginger, garlic and water to a smooth paste in a food processor

2. Seal and brown the meat in the oil. Remove from pan and reserve

3. Add cardamom pods, bay leaves, cloves, pepper, cinnamon and onions

4. Return the meat and juices to the pan. Stir in the yogurt, 1 tbsp at a time

5. Gradually add ½ pint/300 ml water, bring to the boil, stirring, then simmer

6. Skim off any excess oil from the top of the thickened Roghan Josh

CASSOULET

Tasty chunks of bacon, lamb and sausages are combined with haricot beans, vegetables and herbs, then simmered until tender, to create this delicious traditional French dish. Make it as a mouthwatering main meal for lunch or supper.

1. Place washed beans in a large bowl, cover with water and soak overnight

2. Add bacon, carrots, onion, tomatoes, garlic and bouquet garni to the pan

3. Trim lamb and cut into cubes, then melt fat in a second pan and brown meat

1 lb/450 g dried haricot beans

8 oz/225 g piece smoked bacon,
    rind removed

2 small carrots, peeled

1 small onion, peeled and studded
    with 2-3 cloves

8 medium tomatoes

4 garlic cloves, peeled

1 bay leaf

1 parsley sprig

2 thyme sprigs

1 lb/450 g boneless lamb, such
    as fillet

2 oz/50 g lard or white
    vegetable fat

1 medium onion

salt and freshly ground
    black pepper

1 tbsp freshly chopped thyme

2 large pork sausages, quartered

6 oz/175 g garlic sausage,
    thickly sliced

4 oz/100 g white breadcrumbs

flat-leaved parsley to garnish

Preheat the oven to Gas 3, 325°F, 160°C, 10 mins before baking the Cassoulet. Wash the beans, then cover in cold water and leave to soak overnight. Drain beans, then place in a large pan with the bacon, carrots and studded onion. Peel and chop 4 tomatoes, then crush 2 garlic cloves and add to the pan. Tie the bay leaf, parsley and thyme sprigs together to make a bouquet garni, then add to the pan with 3 pints/1.7 litres water. Bring to the boil, then cover and simmer for 1-1½ hrs, or until the beans are tender.

Meanwhile, trim lamb, discarding fat, and cut into cubes. Melt 1 oz/25 g fat in another large pan, add lamb and brown. Peel and slice the onion, finely chop 1 of the remaining garlic cloves, then add to the pan and cook for 3-4 mins. Add ½ pint/300 ml water. Peel and chop the remaining tomatoes, then add to the pan with seasoning and thyme. Bring to the boil, cover and simmer for 1½ hrs.

Melt the remaining fat in a pan and brown the quartered sausages. Drain, then add to the lamb with the garlic sausage for the last 10 mins of cooking time.

Remove beans from the heat, discard

HANDY TIPS

You can use dried red kidney beans instead of haricot beans. After soaking, place in pan, cover with water and boil vigorously for 10 mins. Drain, add bacon and rest of ingredients. Or use canned beans then there is no need to soak or cook first. Add carrots, onions, tomatoes and garlic to the lamb, before cooking.

herbs, carrots and onion. Remove the bacon joint and cut into chunks. Rub the inside of a 4 pint/2.25 litre oven-proof casserole with the remaining peeled garlic clove. Place half of the beans in the base of the casserole. Top with lamb mixture and the bacon, then cover with the remaining beans. Sprinkle 2 oz/50 g breadcrumbs over and bake, uncovered, for 1½ hrs, stirring occasionally to prevent a crust forming, sprinkling each time with more breadcrumbs. When all the bread-crumbs have been used, increase oven temperature to Gas 4, 350°F, 180°C, 25 mins before end of cooking time, so that the top turns golden. Garnish and serve with salad.

4. Add chopped tomatoes, seasoning and thyme, cover and simmer for 1½ hrs

5. Place half the beans in casserole, top with meat, cover with remaining beans

6. Bake, uncovered, for 1½ hrs, stirring occasionally to prevent crust forming

CROWN ROAST OF LAMB

You can't fail to impress dinner guests when you serve this king of roasts. These tender lamb cutlets with a mouth-watering apricot stuffing are just great when you want to cook something special.

Calories per portion: 750   **SERVES 6**

2 racks best end of neck of lamb, 6 or 7 cutlets on each rack
oil for brushing
salt and freshly ground black pepper
6 oz/175 g no-need-to-soak dried apricots
1 onion, peeled and chopped
8 oz/225 g white breadcrumbs
grated rind and juice of 1 orange
2-3 tsp freshly chopped parsley
1 egg, beaten, size 3
14 oz/397 g can apricot halves, drained

Preheat the oven to Gas 5, 375°F, 190°C. Wipe the meat and remove the fat from the top 2 in/5 cm of the thin ends of the bones. Scrape the tops of each bone clean with a knife. Starting from the base of the racks, make a cut upwards between each bone, stopping about a third of the way up from the base. Trim off any excess fat.

Turn the joints inwards so that the bones are on the outside and the meat on the inside, forming both pieces into half circles to join into a crown. Using a trussing needle and string, sew the pieces together at the joints. The thick ends of the meat will make the base of the crown, so check that the base stands level. Place the meat in a baking tin, brush with a little oil and season with plenty of salt and pepper.

To make the stuffing, roughly chop the apricots with a sharp knife or scissors. Place the apricots, chopped onion and breadcrumbs in a bowl. Add the orange rind and parsley and season well. Gradually add the egg and enough orange juice to bind the stuffing. (You will need approximately 1-2 tbsp orange juice, but this can vary.) Spoon the stuffing into the centre cavity of the crown. Roll remaining stuffing into balls.

Wrap small pieces of foil around each piece of bare bone to prevent scorching and place a piece of foil over the top of the stuffing. Weigh the roast and cook in the centre of the oven for 10-15 mins per 1 lb/450 g plus a further 15 mins. Place the stuffing balls round the meat for the last 25 mins of cooking.

When cooked, place the crown on a

serving platter. Remove foil and top each bone with a cutlet frill. Place each stuffing ball in a canned apricot half.

1. Prepare the ingredients and ensure you have a sharp knife for cutting meat

2. Scrape the ends of the cutlet bones clean with a small, sharp knife

3. Sew the two racks firmly together with needle and string to form a crown

4. Mix the stuffing ingredients together, binding well with orange juice

5. Place the stuffing in the centre cavity of the crown, rolling the extra into small balls

6. Cover the ends of each cutlet bone with foil — this will prevent unsightly scorching

LAMB EN CROUTE

Tender cutlets of lamb with a delicious lemon and mint stuffing, encased in crisp, golden puff pastry. This dish is the perfect answer for a special lunch or dinner party. It's impressive, but so easy to make with this step-by-step guide.

Calories per portion: 1,160   **SERVES 4**

best end of lamb joint, with
    8 cutlets (ask butcher to
    chine them)
I small onion
4 button mushrooms
I oz/25 g butter or margarine
2 oz/50 g fresh white
    breadcrumbs
I tbsp freshly chopped mint
grated rind of ½ lemon
salt and freshly ground
    black pepper
I egg, size 3, beaten
I lb/450 g prepared puff pastry
sprigs of fresh mint to garnish
cutlet frills (optional)

Preheat grill. Preheat oven to Gas 7, 425°F, 220°C, 15 mins before cooking. Place lamb on a chopping board. Remove the bone at base of meat, discard any fat. With a small sharp knife, trim meat and fat away from bone at top end of joint to a depth of 2 in/5 cm. Clean bones well.

Peel and finely chop the onion. Wipe and chop mushrooms. Melt butter or margarine in a small pan, then fry onion for 5 mins until soft and transparent. Add the mushrooms and fry for a further minute. Remove from heat. Stir in the breadcrumbs, mint, lemon rind and seasoning to taste. Mix well, then bind with sufficient egg to form a stiff mixture. Reserve remaining egg. Allow stuffing to cool.

Place the cutlets under the preheated grill and brown on both sides. Remove and drain on absorbent paper until cold. Roll out the pastry on a lightly floured surface and cut into eight squares, large enough to encase the cutlets. Reserve trimmings. Place chops on the pastry so that the bone protrudes over the edge of the pastry. Place a spoonful of the stuffing on the centre of the meat. Dampen pastry edges with water, then wrap round, completely encasing each cutlet.

Place on dampened baking sheet with the join underneath. Roll out trimmings and use to decorate the cutlets. Brush pastry with reserved egg, then bake in oven for 10 mins. Brush again with egg, then continue to cook for a further 15-20 mins, or until risen and golden. Turn over and cook underside for 5-7 mins, or until golden. Remove from oven and garnish with mint sprigs. If liked, place cutlet frills on the exposed bones before serving. Serve with freshly cooked vegetables or salad.

HANDY TIP

Roast a boned stuffed leg of lamb for 1½-2 hrs. Cool, then encase in puff pastry, brush with egg and cook at Gas 6, 400°F, 200°C for 40-50 mins.

1. Carefully cut the bone away from the base of the meat with a sharp knife

2. After trimming down the bones at the top, cut into individual cutlets

3. Add the dry ingredients to the onion and mushrooms and bind with beaten egg

4. Grill the chops on both sides until browned, then drain on absorbent paper

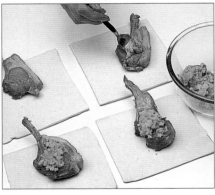

5. Place the chops on pastry squares and spoon stuffing on to centre of meat

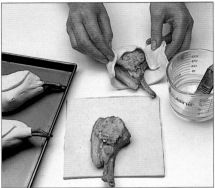

6. Dampen the edges of the pastry with water, then wrap around to encase meat

PORK ESCALOPES

Succulent pieces of pork, spiced with pepper-corns and coated in breadcrumbs, then served with a creamy walnut sauce. This dish is so easy to make and so delicious, too, it's perfect when you want to serve something special.

Calories per portion: 595   SERVES 4

4 x 4 oz/100 g pork steaks

2 tbsp mixed peppercorns, such
    as pink, green and black

2 tbsp flour

salt

1 egg, size 3

6 oz/175 g fresh, fine white
    breadcrumbs

2 oz/50 g unsalted butter

FOR THE WALNUT SAUCE:

½ oz/15 g unsalted butter

2 oz/50 g walnut pieces

1 oz/25 g Parmesan
    cheese, grated

¼ pint/150 ml single cream

1 tbsp lemon juice

salt and freshly ground
    black pepper

lime slices and flat-leaved parsley
    to garnish

Trim the pork, then place between 2 pieces of clear wrap and, using a meat mallet, beat until flattened. Place the peppercorns in a pestle and mortar, and crush. Press the crushed peppercorns on to both sides of the pork.

Place the flour in a shallow dish and season with the salt. Coat the pork steaks in seasoned flour, ensuring that they are completely covered. Beat the egg with 1 tbsp cold water and place in a shallow dish. Place the breadcrumbs in another shallow dish.

Dip the pork in the beaten egg, allow any excess egg to drip off, then completely coat the meat in the breadcrumbs. Melt butter in a frying pan and fry the pork for 5-8 mins on both sides, or until golden and cooked through. Drain well on kitchen paper

HANDY TIPS

For an extra special occasion, add 2 tsp brandy to the sauce with the walnuts. The sauce also makes an excellent starter if mixed into freshly cooked tagliatelle, then sprinkled with extra Parmesan cheese.

and keep warm while preparing the walnut sauce.

To make the sauce, clean the pan with some kitchen paper, then add the butter. Roughly chop the walnuts, add to the pan and cook for 2-3 mins. Stir in the cheese, then the cream, and cook, stirring throughout, for 2-3 mins. Stir in the lemon juice and season to taste. Garnish the escalopes and serve.

1. Trim the pork, place between clearwrap, then beat with a meat mallet until flattened

2. Crush peppercorns in a pestle and mortar, then press on to both sides of the pork steaks

3. Season the flour, then coat the pork in the flour, ensuring all the pieces are completely covered

4. Dip the pork in beaten egg, allow any excess egg to drip off, then coat in the fresh breadcrumbs

5. Fry the escalopes in the melted butter for 5-8 mins on both sides, or until golden and cooked through

6. Cook the roughly chopped walnuts in butter for 2-3 mins. Stir in cheese and cream, then season

PORK CHOPS IN CIDER

Marinating meat before cooking makes it tender and flavoursome and this recipe for Pork Chops in Cider is no exception. The juniper berries and bay leaves give a subtle, yet aromatic flavour to this country-style dish.

Calories per portion: 707 **SERVES 4**

- 2 tbsp juniper berries
- 2 bay leaves
- 3½ tbsp olive oil
- ½ tsp paprika
- 4 tbsp clear honey
- 1 tbsp tomato purée
- 1 pint/600 ml dry cider
- salt and freshly ground
    black pepper
- 4 pork loin chops, each about
    6 oz/175 g in weight
- 2-3 tsp cornflour
- 7 oz/197 g can pineapple pieces
    in natural juice, drained
- 1 tbsp caster sugar
- 2 eating apples, cored, peeled
    and cut into rings

Crush the juniper berries and bay leaves using a pestle and mortar, then mix with 3 tbsp olive oil, the paprika, honey, tomato purée, 18 fl oz/500 ml cider and seasoning. Remove the rind and excess fat from the chops, place in a shallow dish and pour the marinade over them. Cover and leave to marinate in a cool place for 3-4 hours, turning the chops occasionally.

Preheat grill. Remove the chops from the marinade, drain. Cook under a moderately hot grill for 6-8 minutes each side, until well done. Brush frequently with marinade.

When cooked, place on a hot serving dish, cover and keep warm. Strain marinade into a saucepan, bring to the boil, continue boiling until marinade is reduced by half. Mix cornflour with 1 tbsp water, stir into marinade with pineapple and cook, stirring throughout until thickened.

Heat remaining oil in a wide shallow frying pan, sprinkle in caster sugar and continue cooking until sugar turns golden. Add the apple rings and turn them quickly in the caramel to brown lightly. Pour in remaining cider, bring to the boil, reduce, heat and simmer for 2-3 mins until apples are softened.

To serve, pour the cider and pineapple sauce over the chops, then garnish with apple rings. Serve with new potatoes, tossed in parsley, and a crisp green salad.

Alternatively serve with freshly cooked long grain rice, flavoured with cinnamon and stir-fried vegetables.

HANDY TIPS

If you do not have a pestle and mortar, put the juniper berries and bay leaves into a small polythene bag and crush them with a rolling pin. Also, instead of loin chops, you could use chump chops, or try pork tenderloin.

1. Crush juniper berries and bay leaves, mix marinade ingredients together

2. Pour marinade over chops and leave covered to marinate for 3-4 hours

3. Remove chops, drain, then cook under a moderately hot preheated grill

4. Strain remaining marinade into a saucepan and boil until reduced by half

5. Mix cornflour and water, stir into marinade with pineapple. Heat through

6. Poach the prepared apple rings in cider and sugar and use to garnish chops

BAKED GAMMON

Lean, tender and full of goodness-gammon has that special cut-and-come-again appeal. This recipe gives it a crisp and crunchy topping which you can vary according to your taste – try orange, lemon or even glazed with honey.

Calories per portion: 894

SERVES 10

**5 lb/2.25 kg joint gammon,
preferably unsmoked**

2 large onions, peeled

approx 40 cloves

10 black peppercorns

2 carrots, peeled

2 bay leaves

3 oz/75 g demerara sugar

grated rind of 1 orange

Preheat oven to Gas 6, 400°F, 200°C, 15 mins before baking gammon.

If the gammon is smoked, soak it overnight, immersed in cold water. Drain.

Place gammon in a large saucepan, and again cover with fresh cold water. Stud each of the onions with 6 cloves and add to the saucepan with the peppercorns, carrots and bay leaves. Bring to the boil, then with a draining spoon, remove any scum that rises to the surface. Lower the heat, cover then simmer gently. To calculate the cooking time allow 20-25 mins per 1 lb/450 g plus an extra 20 mins. Then simmer the joint for half the cooking time. Allow to cool in the cooking liquid for approximately 1 hr.

Remove the joint from the pan, then

HANDY TIPS

Replace the orange rind with lemon rind or try substituting a 6½ oz/185 g jar of cranberry orange sauce for the demerara sugar and orange – just spoon over the top of the joint 30 mins before end of cooking time. Or pour 3 tbsp of clear honey over the clove-studded gammon, adding 3 tbsp water to the roasting tin before baking, basting with the liquid during cooking.

with a sharp knife carefully strip away the rind. If necessary remove string if used.

With a sharp knife make ⅛ in/3 mm deep cuts at ½ in/1.25 cm intervals across the fat. Then stud each diamond shape with a clove, using a skewer to make a hole if you have difficulty in inserting the cloves.

Mix the demerara sugar with the grated orange rind, then carefully pat into the fat, pressing firmly with the back of a spoon.

Cover the joint lightly with foil, then bake in the oven for the remainder of the calculated cooking time, but remove foil for the last 20 mins. Serve on a platter with seasonal vegetables.

1. *Place gammon in a pan large enough to cover joint with water. Add onions*

2. *When removing scum, take care not to remove the peppercorns or bay leaves*

3. *Carefully strip away the rind to expose the fat and trim away any excess fat*

4. *Make cuts ⅛ in/3 mm deep into the fat at ½ in/1.25 cm intervals across the joint*

5. *Firmly insert a clove into each diamond shape, across top and down the sides*

6. *Cover fat well with demerara sugar, pressing down firmly with back of spoon*

FIDGET PIE

An all-time favourite country pie, full of tender sweet gammon, apples and cider, topped with superlight pastry. Serve it with freshly cooked vegetables for a really filling lunch or supper-time treat.

Calories per portion: 531 **SERVES 6**

FOR THE PASTRY:
8 oz/225 g plain white flour
2 oz/50 g butter or margarine
2 oz/50 g lard or vegetable fat
FOR THE FILLING:
1 lb/450 g tender-sweet gammon
1 small onion
2 small cooking apples
juice of 1 lemon
salt and freshly ground
black pepper
2 oz/50 g plain flour
¼ pint/150 ml medium dry cider
or vegetable stock
1 egg, size 5, beaten

Preheat oven to Gas 6, 400°F, 200°C. Sift the flour into a mixing bowl. Cut the fat into cubes, add to the flour and rub in with fingertips until the mixture resembles fine breadcrumbs. Mix to a firm but pliable dough with 4-6 tbsp cold water. Knead until smooth and free from cracks, wrap and leave in fridge while preparing filling.

Cut the gammon into ½ in/1.25 cm strips, discard fat and dice.

Peel and finely chop the onion. Place gammon and onion in a large mixing bowl. Peel the cooking apples, cut into quarters and discard cores. Dice the apple, then sprinkle with lemon juice. Add to the gammon with seasoning to taste. (Take care how much salt you use, especially if the gammon is smoked. If so, you'll only need pepper.)

Roll out the pastry on a lightly floured surface, invert a 2 pint/1.2 litre pie dish on top and cut out lid. Roll the trimmings and cut out a 1 in/2.5 cm strip, long enough to go round the pie dish. Dampen the pie dish edge and place strip round. Place the filling in the dish, ensuring that it is evenly distributed. Blend the flour with the cider or stock to a smooth paste, then pour over the filling. Dampen the edges of the pastry strip with cold water. Wrap the pastry lid around rolling pin and position.

Seal edges firmly, then flute together with back of a round-bladed knife. Make a decorative pattern around the edge. Cut a diagonal cross in the centre of the lid then fold the pastry back to reveal the filling. Use any trimmings to decorate the lid, and brush with beaten egg. Bake in the oven for 20 mins. Reduce oven temperature to Gas 4, 350°F, 180°C, brush again with beaten egg, return to oven and cook for a further 20-25 mins or until the pastry is golden brown.

HANDY tips

If liked, the gammon can be replaced with back bacon. Try using no-need-to-soak dried apricots instead of the apples.

1. Cut the gammon into ½ in/1.25 cm strips and discard any fat, then dice

2. Peel and chop onion, place in a bowl with gammon. Peel, core and dice apples

3. Roll pastry out on a lightly floured surface, invert pie dish and cut out lid

4. Place filling into dish, blend flour with cider or stock and pour over

5. Dampen pastry strip, wrap lid round rolling pin and carefully place in position

6. Seal pastry edges, making a pattern, cut a cross in centre and turn back

PORK CHASSEUR

Tender strips of pork fillet with green and red peppers, button mushrooms that are all gently simmered in white wine and served with freshly cooked white and green tagliatelle. It's so easy to prepare and cook.

Calories per portion: 746   SERVES 4

1½ lb/675 g pork fillet

12 juniper berries

1 large onion

1 green pepper

1 red pepper

6 oz/175 g button mushrooms

3-4 tbsp vegetable oil

½ pint/300 ml white wine

½ pint/300 ml pork or
    vegetable stock

salt and freshly ground
    black pepper

2 bay leaves

1½ oz/40 g butter or margarine

1½ oz/40 g flour

freshly cooked white and green
    tagliatelle to serve

Preheat oven to Gas 4, 350°F, 180°C. Discard any fat from pork and cut into strips 2 in/5 cm long x ½ in/1.25 cm thick. Place juniper berries in a pestle and mortar and crush lightly. Alternatively, place them in a polythene bag and crush with a rolling pin. Reserve.

Peel onion, slice thinly. Deseed green and red peppers, slice thinly into rings. Wipe or wash and dry the mushrooms.

HANDY TIP

Juniper berries are small black berries, obtainable from major supermarkets and delicatessens. They are crushed lightly to help the extraction of their fragrance and aroma. They have a slightly woody, smoky flavour and are used in the making of gin.

Heat the oil in a large frying pan then fry the pork until browned on all sides. Drain, using a slotted spoon and place in a 4 pint/2.25 litre ovenproof casserole dish. Lightly fry the juniper berries in the remaining oil for 1 min. Add the sliced onion and peppers and then continue to fry for a further 5 mins or until onion is transparent and soft. Pour in wine and stock with seasoning to taste. Bring to the boil then pour over the pork. Add the bay leaves, cover and cook in the oven for 1½-2 hrs or until pork is tender.

Half an hour before end of cooking time, fry the mushrooms in ½ oz/15 g of the butter or margarine, drain, then add to casserole. When pork is cooked, discard bay leaves and pour liquid into small saucepan. Arrange the pork and vegetables on serving dish and keep warm.

Cream the remaining butter or margarine and flour together to form beurre manié. Boil cooking liquid for 5 mins, then reduce heat and whisk in small spoonfuls of the beurre manié until sauce is smooth and thickened. Pour over the pork and vegetables and serve with the freshly cooked white and green tagliatelle.

1. Discard fat then cut pork tenderloin into 2 in x ½ in/5 cm x 1.25 cm strips

2. Lightly crush the juniper berries in a pestle and mortar to extract the flavour

3. Peel, thinly slice onion, deseed peppers, slice. Wash and dry mushrooms

4. Heat oil, fry pork until browned all over. Transfer to an ovenproof casserole

5. Fry onion and peppers for 5 mins, or until onion is soft. Add the wine

6. Place stock in saucepan. Whisk in small amounts of beurre manié until thickened

ROAST STUFFED PORK

Slices of roast pork, nutty stuffing flavoured with peaches and fresh herbs and crisp golden crackling create this mouthwatering treat; ideal for a perfect Sunday lunch.

3 oz/75 g dried peaches

3 lb/1.5k g pork joint, boned and scored

1 oz/25 g half-fat butter

1 small onion

1 stick celery

4 oz/100 g fresh white breadcrumbs

2 oz/50 g pine kernels

1½ tbsp freshly chopped parsley and rosemary, mixed together

1 egg, size 5

oil for brushing

2 tbsp coarse rock salt

HANDY TIPS

Standing the pork on a trivet or rack helps greatly in achieving crisp crackling. When carving, cut the string and discard. Cut crackling off first and divide into portions. This makes the joint easier to carve.

The best joints to use are: boned and rolled loin; boned half leg; and boned and rolled hand and spring.

For a change, try serving the apple sauce in drained, canned peach halves.

Preheat oven to Gas 4, 350°F, 180°C. Place dried peaches in a small saucepan, cover with boiling water. Cook over a gentle heat for 10 mins. Drain, allow to cool then chop. Wipe pork with a clean damp cloth and leave joint in fridge while preparing stuffing.

Melt fat in a saucepan. Peel and finely chop the onion. Trim, scrub then finely chop the celery. Cook the onion and celery in the melted fat for 5 mins or until soft and transparent but not browned. Remove from heat. Stir in the chopped peaches, breadcrumbs, pine kernels and herbs. Season to taste. Add the egg and mix the stuffing to a stiff consistency.

Lay the pork out on a clean surface or chopping board, rind side down. Place stuffing in the centre of the joint, packing it down firmly. Roll the meat up and secure with string, encasing the stuffing as much as possible. Tie the joint in several places to help keep its shape during cooking.

Weigh joint then calculate cooking time allowing 30 mins per 1 lb/450 g, plus 30 mins. Place joint on a trivet or rack and stand in a roasting tin. Brush rind with oil, then sprinkle with freshly ground rock salt.

Place on centre shelf of oven and cook for the calculated time. Thirty mins before the end of the cooking, remove from oven and grind more salt over the rind to give a really crisp crackling. Allow joint to stand for at least 5 mins before carving. Use juices from tin to make gravy.

1. Melt the fat in the pan and gently fry the onion and celery for 5 mins

2. Bind all the stuffing ingredients to a stiff consistency with the egg

3. Place the stuffing in the centre of the joint, packing it down firmly

4. Tie the joint securely in several places to keep its shape during cooking

5. Place the joint on a trivet or rack in a roasting tin. Brush with oil

6. For a crisp crackling, grind rock salt over the rind before and during cooking

ORIENTAL PORK

Succulent strips of pork gently cooked in sherry and soy sauce with colourful crunchy peppers and water chestnuts give this casserole a taste of the Orient. Serve it for a special occasion or as a family meal.

1 small red pepper, washed
1 small green pepper, washed
1 small yellow pepper, washed
1½ lb/675 g lean pork, preferably
    from leg, spare rib or fillet
2 in/5 cm piece root ginger
1 large onion
2 tbsp vegetable oil
2 tbsp soy sauce
¼ pint/150 ml dry sherry
1-2 tsp Chinese five spice powder
¾ pint/450 ml pork or
    vegetable stock
7 oz/227 g can water chestnuts
1 oz/25 g butter or margarine
1 oz/25 g plain flour
spring onion tassels to garnish
freshly cooked Chinese egg
    noodles and stir fried
    vegetables to serve

Preheat oven to Gas 4, 350°F, 180°C. Cut the tops off peppers, discard seeds, cut in half lengthways, then into strips about ¼ in/6 mm thick. Discard fat and bones from pork, cut into 1 in/2.5 cm slices then cut into strips about 3 in/7.5 cm long x ½ in/1.25 cm wide. Thinly peel root ginger, then either grate or chop finely. Peel the onion and slice thinly.

Heat oil then gently fry the onion for 5 mins or until soft and transparent. Transfer to ovenproof casserole using a draining spoon. Add pork and grated ginger to oil remaining in pan and fry until meat is brown. Turn heat down, add the soy sauce, sherry, Chinese five spice powder and stock. Bring slowly to boil then pour into casserole dish. Cover and cook in oven for 1 hr or until pork is just tender.

Place peppers into large bowl, pour over boiling water to cover and leave for 2 mins. Drain thoroughly, then add to casserole, together with drained water chestnuts. Continue to cook for a further 15 mins.

Beat the butter or margarine with the flour to a beurre manié. Pour off the liquid into a small saucepan and bring to a slow boil. Drop small amounts of beurre manié into liquid and whisk vigorously until sauce is thick and smooth. Check seasoning, then pour over cooked pork and peppers.

Mix well, arrange on a warmed serving dish. Serve immediately with freshly cooked Chinese egg noodles, decorated with a spring onion tassel, stir-fried vegetables such as strips of carrot, mangetout, baby corn and bean sprouts, and extra soy sauce.

HANDY TIP

For a change, add mushrooms – oyster or chanterelle are usually available. Clean, fry lightly in oil, drain and add to casserole with the peppers and water chestnuts.

1. Cut top from peppers, discard seeds and cut in half. Cut into thin strips

2. Trim pork, discard fat and bone. Cut into 1 in/2.5 cm slices then thin strips

3. Thinly peel root ginger with small kitchen knife, then grate or chop

4. Fry sliced onion in oil. Using draining spoon transfer to casserole

5. Using wooden spoon, fry pork and ginger in remaining oil until brown

6. Turn heat to very low, add soy sauce, sherry, five spice powder and stock

FISH CASSEROLE

Try this unusual combination of tender pieces of moist fish and lightly cooked vegetables, braised in beer and served in a delicious creamy sauce. Ideal for a quick and easy mid week supper dish.

Calories per portion: 512   SERVES 4

8 oz/225 g baby onions

8 oz/225 g carrots

2 celery sticks

6 oz/175 g courgettes

1½ lb/675 g huss fillets
or monkfish

1½ tbsp seasoned flour

3 tbsp sunflower oil

2 bay leaves

½ pint/300 ml light ale

¼ pint/150 ml fish or
vegetable stock

1½ oz/40 g butter or margarine

1½ oz/40 g plain flour

4 tbsp single cream

fresh chervil sprigs to garnish

Preheat oven to Gas 4, 350°F, 180°C, 10 mins before cooking the casserole. Peel the onions and carrots then cut carrots in half then into chunks approx 1 in/2.5cm in length. Wash and trim celery, cut into 1 in/2.5cm chunks.

Wash and trim courgettes, cut in half then into 1 in/2.5cm chunks.

Skin fish if necessary then cut off and discard the central bone. (If using huss this is slightly to one side of the fillet. If using monkfish, the bone is located down the centre.) Wash and dry the fillets then cut into 1½ in/4 cm chunks. Coat lightly in the seasoned flour.

Heat 2 tbsp of the oil in a frying pan then gently fry the onions, carrot and celery for 10 mins. Add the courgettes and fry for a further 1 min. Drain well and place in the base of a 4 pint/ 2.25 litre ovenproof casserole. Add the remaining oil to the pan then lightly fry the fish for approx 4 mins turning the pieces over at least once. Drain then add to the casserole. Pour in the ale and stock then add the bay leaves. Cover and cook in the oven for 30-35 mins or until the fish and vegetables are cooked.

Remove from the oven and carefully drain off the liquid, discarding the bay leaves. Keep the fish and vegetables hot while thickening the sauce with the beurre manié.

Beat the fat and flour together in a small bowl and strain the liquid into a small pan. Place over the heat and bring to the boil. Drop small spoonfuls of the beurre manié into the boiling liquid, whisk vigorously. Once all the beurre manié has been used and the sauce thickened, remove from the heat, adjust seasoning then stir in the cream. Pour over the fish and vegetables and serve.

HANDY TIP

Look out for huss, whiting or pollack at your local fishmongers, they are cheaper than prime cod, haddock or monkfish and just as delicious.

1. Prepare the baby onions, carrots, celery sticks and courgettes and cut into 1 in/2.5 cm chunks

2. Discard bones from the fish, cut into 1½ in/4 cm chunks then coat in the seasoned flour

3. Heat 2 tbsp of the oil in a frying pan then fry the onions, celery and carrots for 10 mins. Place vegetables in casserole

4. Add the remaining oil to pan, then lightly fry the fish for 4 mins, turning the pieces over at least once

5. Add fish and bay leaves to the casserole, then pour the ale and stock over

6. Bring the cooking liquid to the boil, add small spoonfuls of the beurre manié, and whisk

GOLDEN FISH PIE

Try this appetizing dish of delicious chunks of cod mixed with smoked haddock and prawns in a creamy sauce, then wrapped in golden puff pastry. This dish is a delight for all the family.

Calories per portion: 117   **SERVES 4**

10 oz/300 g cod fillets

10 oz/300 g smoked haddock fillets

¾ pint/450 ml milk

2 bay leaves

5 green peppercorns

5 black peppercorns

small bunch of parsley

2 oz/50 g butter or margarine

3 oz/75 g plain flour

salt and freshly ground black pepper

3 oz/75 g peeled prawns

1 lb/450 g puff pastry, thawed if frozen

1 egg, beaten, size 3

Preheat the oven to Gas 7, 425°F, 220°C, 15 mins before cooking pie. Place all the fish on a board and using a sharp knife skin the fish by holding the end of each fillet and cutting off as much flesh as possible with a sawing motion. (If you don't have a very sharp knife or find this difficult it's well worth asking the fishmonger to remove the skin for you.)

Cut the cod and haddock into small pieces. Place the milk in a frying pan or saucepan with the bay leaves, green and black peppercorns and a sprig of

HANDY TIP

For a special occasion use fresh salmon instead of the smoked haddock and add two size 3 eggs, hard-boiled, shelled and chopped.

parsley. Add the fish to the milk and simmer for 6 mins. Strain the liquid from the pan and reserve.

Place the fat in a saucepan and heat gently until melted. Add the flour and stir over a gentle heat for 2 mins, until the fat and flour form a ball in the base of the saucepan. Remove from heat and gradually stir in the reserved milk to make a smooth sauce. Return to the heat, bring to boil and simmer for 5 mins until sauce has thickened. Season with salt and pepper, remove from the heat and allow to cool.

Stir in the cooked cod, smoked haddock and prawns. Chop the remaining parsley then add to the saucepan and mix well.

Dust a working surface with flour. Roll out pastry to a 12 in/30 cm square. Trim sides with a sharp knife. Pile the fish filling into the centre and brush all the edges of the pastry with water. Bring two corners to the centre of the square so that the two corners and sides meet as shown. Dust fingertips with plenty of flour and pinch the edges together well to seal. Repeat with remaining two corners, pinching all the edges together to encase fish filling in the pastry. Crimp all the edges with your fingers and transfer the pie to a baking sheet and brush well with the beaten egg.

Cook for 30 mins until pastry has risen and is a golden brown colour. Serve this mouthwatering dish garnished with sprigs of parsley and slices of lemon.

1. Prepare, weigh and measure all the ingredients before you begin

2. Cube fish and poach in pan with peppercorns, milk, bay leaf and parsley

3. Gradually add the milk to the pan and beat to a smooth sauce

4. Mix all the filling ingredients into the sauce and season well

5. Spoon filling into centre of pastry square and brush edges with water

6. Fold corners into centre, pinch and flute edges with fingertips

SOLE VERONIQUE

A delicious and impressive dish, the delicate flavour of the sole blends perfectly with the creamy white wine sauce and is complemented by the subtle tang of grapes. An ideal dish for entertaining.

Calories per portion: 387

SERVES 4

8 sole fillets

salt and freshly ground
black pepper

1 small onion, peeled and
thinly sliced

2 mushrooms, wiped and sliced

2-3 bay leaves

juice of ½ lemon

½ pint/300 ml dry white wine

4 oz/100 g white grapes,
preferably seedless

FOR THE SAUCE:

¼ pint/150 ml milk

1½ oz/40g butter or margarine

1½ oz/40 g flour

1 egg yolk, size 3

¼ pint/150 ml single cream

TO GARNISH:

few parsley sprigs

4 lemon slices

Preheat oven to Gas 4, 350°F, 180°C, 10 mins before cooking fish. Lay each fish fillet flesh side down on a chopping board, with tail end towards you. With a sharp knife loosen the skin from the flesh at the tail end. Grasp the skin with the fingertips and pull it off from the tail to the head. Trim the edges with a sharp knife.

Wash then pat dry with absorbent paper and season with salt and pepper. Roll the fillets up, starting from the tail end, and place in a baking tin or shallow ovenproof dish.

Scatter the onion, mushroom slices and bay leaves over the top, mix the lemon juice, ¼ pint/150 ml of the white wine and ¼ pint/150 ml of water together, then pour over the fish. Cover closely with foil. Cook for 15 mins or until fish is cooked.

Meanwhile, place the grapes in a small pan with the remaining ¼ pint/ 150 ml of the wine and simmer gently for 5 mins. Drain, then peel.

Arrange the cooked fish on a serving dish, reserving the liquid, and keep fish warm while making sauce.

Make up the milk to 8 fl oz/250 ml with fish liquid.

Melt the butter or margarine in a small pan, add flour and cook for 2 mins. Draw the pan off the heat and gradually stir in the milk and fish liquid. Return to the heat and cook gently, stirring throughout until the mixture thickens. Draw off the heat again, then beat in the egg yolk and the cream with

1. Trim the fillets of sole, discarding any bones and small pieces of skin

3. Thinly slice onions and mushrooms and scatter over the rolled sole fillets

5. While making the sauce, simmer the grapes in the wine for a few mins

HANDY TIPS

If you like, plaice fillets can be used instead of sole. Always eat fish the day it's cooked.

seasoning to taste.

Add most of the grapes, reserving a few for decoration, then heat through gently until hot. Pour a little over the fillets and serve the remaining sauce in a sauceboat. Decorate with reserved grapes, parsley sprigs and lemon slices.

2. Carefully roll the fillets up tucking the ends in to make neat fish parcels

4. Mix the lemon juice, wine and water then pour over the fillets. Season well

6. Add the peeled grapes to the finished sauce, reserving a few for decoration

SALMON EN CROUTE

Tempting flakes of fresh salmon in a creamy white wine sauce, encased in crisp golden puff pastry, a really impressive dish, ideal for all the family. It's easy to make if you follow the step-by-step guide.

Calories per portion: 544   SERVES 8

1 lb/450 g piece tail-end
   of salmon
1 small onion, peeled and sliced
small piece of carrot, peeled
   and chopped
2 bay leaves
few parsley sprigs
¼ pint/150 ml medium-dry
   white wine
1½ oz/40 g butter or margarine
1½ oz/40 g plain flour
salt and freshly ground
   black pepper
1 tbsp freshly chopped dill
grated rind of ½ lemon
¼ pint/150 ml single cream
4 oz/100 g cooked long grain rice
4 oz/100 g peeled
   prawns, optional
1 lb/450 g prepared puff pastry
1 egg, size 5, beaten
lemon and cucumber twists,
   whole prawns and dill sprigs
   to garnish

Preheat the oven to Gas 7, 425°F, 220°C, 15 mins before cooking. Remove scales from salmon, then wash well in cold water and pat dry. Place salmon in frying pan with onion, carrot, bay leaves, parsley, wine and ½ pint/300 ml water. Bring to a gentle

HANDY TIPS

Try using other fish, such as haddock or cod fillet instead of the salmon. You can also use fish stock instead of white wine.

boil, then simmer for 10-15 mins. Remove from heat, cover and cool. Strain cooking liquid and reserve ½ pint/300 ml. Skin, bone and flake salmon. Cover and reserve.

Melt fat in a saucepan, add flour and cook for 2 mins. Lower heat, then stir in the reserved cooking liquid, mixing well. Cook for a further minute until thick, smooth and glossy. Remove from the heat and stir in seasoning, dill, lemon rind, cream and rice. Mix well, then add prawns if using, and salmon. Leave until cold. Meanwhile, cut the pastry in half, then roll out into two oblongs, approx 13 in × 9 in/33 cm × 23 cm. With a round-bladed knife mark out on one the outline of a fish.

Place filling inside the fish shape and brush edges with cold water. Place the other oblong on top and press edges to seal. Using a pastry wheel, cut out fish, ¼ in/6 mm away from edge of filling. Knock up edges with a knife.

Roll out trimmings and, using a small plain round cutter, stamp out scales. Brush with beaten egg and position on fish, starting at the tail and overlapping as you go. Leave head free and fix one round for the eye. Mark tail with a sharp knife. Place on a baking sheet and brush with beaten egg.

Bake for 20 mins, then lower oven temperature to Gas 4, 350°F, 180°C, and bake for a further 20-25 mins until golden brown and risen. Garnish with lemon and cucumber twists, prawns and dill.

1. Place salmon in pan, with onion, carrot, bay leaves, parsley, wine and water

2. Drain cooked salmon, reserving liquid, then discard skin and bones and flake

3. Melt fat in pan, add flour and cook for 2 mins. Gradually stir in the liquid

4. Mark the shape of a fish on one of the pastry oblongs and add the filling

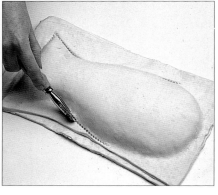

5. Dampen edge, place second oblong on top. Cut out fish shape

6. Brush the small pastry rounds with beaten egg, then place in position

PAUPIETTES OF SOLE

Delicate sole fillets are simply delicious stuffed with a mixture of prawns, mushrooms and pine nuts, gently cooked in white wine with a hint of orange. They make an impressive main meal or starter.

Calories per portion: 274   SERVES 4

4 lemon sole fillets

1 oz/25 g fresh white breadcrumbs

2 spring onions

1½ oz/40 g peeled prawns, thawed if frozen

1 dill sprig

1½ oz/40 g button mushrooms, wiped

1 tbsp pine nuts

salt and freshly ground black pepper

1 egg, size 5

2 bay leaves

¼ pint/150 ml medium-dry white wine, optional

1 orange

¼ pint/150 ml double cream

1 egg yolk, size 3

dill sprigs and orange slices to garnish

Preheat the oven to Gas 4, 350°F, 180°C, 10 mins before cooking the fish. Lightly grease an ovenproof dish. Wash fish under cold water, dry with kitchen paper, then skin.

Place breadcrumbs in a bowl. Trim the spring onions and chop finely, then add to bowl. Dry prawns with kitchen paper and chop. Chop dill and add to the breadcrumbs with the prawns. Chop mushrooms finely, stir into mixture with the pine nuts and seasoning to taste. Bind mixture together with the egg to form a soft but not sticky mixture.

Lay the fillets out on a chopping board and halve lengthways. Divide prepared filling evenly between fillets, spreading it to within ½ in/1.25 cm of each end. Roll up fish, starting from the tail end, then place in the ovenproof dish. Add bay leaves to dish, then pour in the wine and ¼ pint/150 ml water (use all water or fish stock if not using wine). Using a zester, cut approximately 1 tsp of rind from orange, then scatter

rind over fillets.

Cover and cook in preheated oven for 15-18 mins or until cooked. Remove from the oven and drain off the cooking liquid into a saucepan. (Keep the fish hot while preparing the sauce.)

Boil cooking liquid until reduced by half. Beat the cream and egg yolk together, stir into the liquid and continue to cook gently, stirring throughout until sauce is of a creamy consistency. Do not allow the sauce to boil. Adjust the seasoning, then pour round fish and garnish with dill and orange slices.

HANDY TIP

If you're worried about the paupiettes unrolling during cooking, carefully tie them with fine thread or secure with cocktail sticks. Don't forget to remove the thread or sticks before serving.

1. Wash the sole fillets under cold water, dry with kitchen paper, then skin

2. Trim and chop spring onions, add to breadcrumbs. Chop prawns and dill

3. Divide filling evenly between halved fillets to within ½ in/1.25 cm of each end

4. *Starting from the tail end, roll up each fillet, then place in ovenproof dish*

5. *Add bay leaves, pour in wine, ¼ pint/ 150 ml water, scatter orange rind over*

6. *Boil cooking liquid until reduced by half, then stir in cream and egg yolk*

PLAICE FLORENTINE

Tasty plaice fillets filled with a tangy lemon and mustard stuffing and coated with a creamy cheese sauce, served on a bed of chopped spinach. This dish makes an ideal special treat for all the family.

2 large plaice
2 onions, peeled
few bay leaves
1-2 celery stalks, trimmed
few peppercorns
2½ oz/65 g butter or margarine
1 lemon, scrubbed
2 oz/50 g button mushrooms, wiped or washed and chopped
2 oz/50 g fresh white breadcrumbs
1 egg, size 5, beaten
1 lb/450 g cooked spinach
1½ oz/40 g plain flour
½ pint/300 ml milk
2-3 oz/50-75 g Cheddar cheese, grated

Preheat oven to Gas 6, 400°F, 200°C, 15 mins before cooking fish. Ask the fishmonger to fillet and skin the plaice for you. Keep the trimmings. Place the trimmings in a frying pan with one of the onions, sliced, bay leaves, celery, roughly chopped, and the peppercorns. Cover with water, bring to the boil, then simmer gently for 10 mins. Strain and allow the fish stock to cool.

HANDY TIP

This can be prepared to the stage of pouring over the sauce. If doing this store, covered, in a cool place for no more than 6-8 hrs. It will then need longer in the oven to ensure that the fish is thoroughly heated through.

Chop the remaining onion then sweat in 1 oz/25 g butter or margarine until soft and translucent. Remove from the heat. Add grated rind from lemon. Add mushrooms with the breadcrumbs and seasoning. Bind with sufficient egg to give a stiff consistency.

Place the fillets skinned side down and season. Place the prepared stuffing in centre, roll up to form a neat shape. Secure with cocktail sticks. Place in a lightly buttered ovenproof dish, cover with ½ pint/300 ml of the fish stock. Cover with lid or foil and cook in oven for 10-15 mins or until the fillets are just cooked.

Meanwhile, arrange finely chopped spinach in the base of an ovenproof dish and make the sauce. Melt remaining fat in a saucepan, stir in flour and cook for 2 mins. Remove from heat and gradually stir in the milk. Return to heat then cook, stirring throughout until sauce thickens. Remove from heat, add seasoning and cheese, stir until cheese has melted.

Arrange fillets on top of spinach, and discard cocktail sticks. Pour the prepared cheese sauce over then return to the oven to cook for a further 10 mins or until golden brown and bubbly. Serve immediately.

1. Place fish trimmings in pan with onion, bay leaves, celery and peppercorns

2. Sweat chopped onion in fat for 5 mins. Remove from heat, add lemon rind

3. Place stuffing in centre of fillets, roll up, secure with cocktails sticks

4. Pour over the cooled fish stock. Cover with foil, cook for 10-15 mins

5. Transfer the cooked fillets with a slice on to spinach. Discard cocktail sticks

6. Coat fish with cheese sauce, return to oven and cook until golden brown

PAELLA

One of Spain's most popular dishes, paella, packed full of appetizing fish, shellfish, chicken and pork. Paella makes a perfect meal for the whole family or is ideal for an informal supper party.

Calories per portion: 568   **SERVES 6**

1 lb/450 g fresh mussels or
    6 oz/175 g shelled, cooked
    mussels
1½ lb/675 g piece monkfish
1 large red pepper
1 large Spanish onion
2-3 garlic cloves
8 oz/225 g tomatoes
few saffron strands or
    ½-1 tsp turmeric
1 lb/450 g pork tenderloin
12 oz/350 g chicken breasts
2-3 tbsp olive oil
1 sprig rosemary
12 oz/350 g Valencia or
    risotto rice
¼ pint/150 ml dry white wine
1½ pints/900 ml fish stock
salt and freshly ground
    black pepper
3 oz/75 g peas
4 oz/100 g peeled prawns
2 oz/50 g whole prawns

HANDY TIPS

You can vary the ingredients of a paella to suit your palate and availability. Try adding chorizo (a spicy continental sausage), squid, Mediterranean prawns and, for a special occasion, lobster. For a change, cook your Paella over a barbecue – follow the recipe as above, but increase the amount of liquid as it will evaporate when cooked in the open.

Discard beards from the mussels and scrub thoroughly in cold water. Throw away any mussels that are open. Leave covered in a bowl of cold water.

Skin the monkfish, cut down centre and discard bone. Cut the flesh into 1 in/2.5 cm pieces. Wash and dry pepper, deseed then slice thinly. Peel, then finely chop onion. Peel and crush garlic. Wash and dry tomatoes, slice.

Place saffron in a small bowl, pour boiling water over and leave to infuse for at least 10 mins. Trim off any fat or gristle from the pork and chicken, cut in 1 in/2.5 cm pieces.

Heat the oil in a paella pan or large frying pan and fry the meat for 5 mins until browned, stir occasionally. Add the onion, garlic, tomatoes and sliced red pepper.

Lightly crush the sprig of rosemary, add to the pan together with the rice. Cook for 5 mins, stirring to prevent the ingredients sticking to the bottom of the pan. Add the monkfish, white wine and stock with seasoning. Bring to the boil then simmer for 10 mins.

Strain the saffron liquid into the pan (if using turmeric blend with 2 tsp cold water) and add the mussels, peas and peeled prawns and continue cooking for 8 mins or until the rice, meat and fish are cooked and the mussels have opened. Add a little extra stock if the paella is too dry.

Turn off heat, cover with a clean cloth or foil and leave for 3 mins. Discard any mussels that have not opened. Decorate with whole prawns.

1. Discard beards from mussels and scrub in cold water, discard any that are open

2. Skin monkfish, cut down centre, discard central bone, cut into 1 in/2.5 cm pieces

3. Prepare pepper, onion and tomatoes, crush garlic, infuse saffron in water

4. Heat olive oil in pan, fry diced meat until browned all over, stir occasionally

5. Add onion, garlic, tomatoes, rosemary, sliced pepper, stir then pour in the rice

6. After cooking rice, add monkfish and mussels, pour in wine and stock

PASTA WITH BASIL

Add an Italian flavour to your cooking with tasty strips of home-made pasta and courgettes, coated in a creamy sauce that's flavoured with Parmesan cheese and basil. It's ideal for an informal lunch.

10 oz/300 g strong plain
     white flour
pinch of salt
3 eggs, size 1
2 courgettes
FOR THE SAUCE:
1 oz/25 g butter
1 small onion
4 oz/100 g Parmesan cheese,
     freshly grated
½ pint/300 ml double cream
2 tbsp freshly chopped basil
salt and freshly ground
     white pepper
basil sprig

Place the flour in a heap with a large hollow in the centre, on a very clean board or work surface.

Sprinkle the salt into the flour, then break the eggs, one at a time, into the centre. Gradually stir the flour into the eggs using a fork. When it becomes difficult to handle with a fork, use your hands. Mix the flour and eggs to form a pliable dough, adding a little extra flour if the dough becomes too sticky.

Continue to knead the dough, dusting your hands and the surface with a little extra flour as you go, until the dough becomes smooth and elastic.

This should take approx 10-15 mins. (If you have a pasta machine you can put the dough through after the first kneading.) Then, place the dough in a clean bowl, cover it loosely and leave to relax for 30 mins.

On a lightly floured surface, roll out the relaxed dough very thinly and evenly, rolling the dough away from you and rotating it as you go. Roll up, as for a Swiss roll, then cut into strips ¼ in/6 mm wide. Open up strips then leave to dry on a clean tea towel for 10 mins.

Bring a large pan of lightly salted

water to the boil, then cook the pasta for approx 3-4 mins, or until 'al dente'. (A general rule for cooking pasta is to allow 2 pints/1.2 litres of water for every 4 oz/100 g of pasta.) Drain the pasta and keep warm.

Wash and trim the courgettes, then, using a vegetable peeler, shave them into thin strips. Blanch the strips of courgette in boiling salted water for approx 1 min. Drain the strips, refresh in cold water, then drain again. Reserve.

To make the sauce, melt the butter in a large pan. Peel and finely chop the onion, then add to pan and cook gently for 5 mins, or until soft and transparent. Stir in 2 oz/50 g Parmesan cheese and the cream. Add the drained pasta and heat through gently.

When the pasta has been thoroughly heated, stir in the remaining cheese, the chopped basil and courgettes. Season to taste with salt and freshly ground pepper. Heat through for 2-3 mins, stir

HANDY TIP

You can vary the ingredients of this dish – try adding thin strips of smoked ham, sliced, lightly cooked mushrooms or peeled prawns.

gently, then garnish. Serve immediately on a warmed serving dish, accompanied by a salad, fresh crusty bread and extra Parmesan cheese.

1. Pile the flour in a heap, make a large hollow in the centre and add the three eggs one at a time

2. Gradually stir the flour into the eggs with a fork, mix to form a pliable dough, adding extra flour if necessary

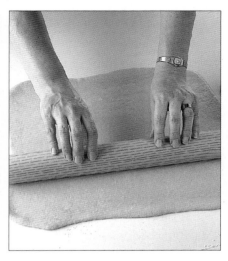

3. Working on a lightly floured surface, roll out the relaxed dough very thinly and evenly

4. Roll up, as for a Swiss roll, then cut into strips ¼ in/6 mm wide, leave to dry for 10 mins

5. Melt butter in pan then fry the onion for 5 mins. Stir in 2 oz/50 g Parmesan cheese

6. Stir the double cream into the onion and cheese, before adding the cooked pasta

CANNELLONI

A delicious combination of grated mozzarella cheese, minced beef and fresh pasta, topped with a smooth, creamy béchamel sauce go to make this classic Italian dish.

Calories per portion: 435   SERVES 6

1 pint/600 ml milk

2 small onions

1 small carrot

1 stick celery

4-5 peppercorns

2-3 fresh bay leaves

1 garlic clove

1 tbsp olive oil

10 oz/300 g lean minced beef

½ small red pepper

½ small green pepper

2 tbsp tomato purée

2 tbsp freshly chopped chervil

salt and freshly ground
    black pepper

¼ pint/150 ml Italian red wine or
    beef stock

4 oz/100 g mozzarella cheese,
    coarsely grated

12 fresh lasagne sheets

12 oz/350 g ripe tomatoes

2 oz/50 g butter or margarine

2 oz/50 g flour

1-2 tbsp Parmesan cheese,
    finely grated

Preheat the oven to Gas 5, 375°F, 190°C, 10 mins before baking the cannelloni. Place the milk in a saucepan. Peel 1 of the onions, peel carrot. Scrub celery, trim and discard ends. Place the onion, carrot and celery into the milk with the peppercorns and bay leaves. Heat gently to just below boiling point. Remove from heat, cover and leave to infuse for 30 mins. Strain, reserving the milk.

Peel and finely chop the remaining onion, peel and crush the garlic. Place in a frying pan with the oil and fry for 5 mins. Add the minced beef and continue to fry, stirring until the meat is browned. Deseed peppers, chop finely. Add to the minced beef and continue to cook for 5 mins. Then add tomato purée, 1 tbsp chervil and seasoning. Pour in wine or stock, cook gently for 10 mins. Cool slightly.

Place small spoonfuls of mozzarella cheese and beef mixture on the pasta sheets then roll up. Continue until

all the sheets have been filled. Slice tomatoes and arrange in base of an ovenproof dish. Sprinkle with remaining chervil and seasoning. Arrange filled pasta on top, keeping the joins underneath.

Melt the butter or margarine in a small saucepan, stir in the flour, cook for 1 min. Remove from heat then gradually stir in the reserved milk. Return pan to heat and cook, stirring, until the sauce thickens. Add seasoning to taste. Pour over the pasta and sprinkle the top with the Parmesan cheese. Cook in the oven for 30-40 mins until golden brown. Serve immediately with a green salad.

HANDY TIP

If you can't buy fresh lasagne sheets, buy dried ones and cook them first, with a little oil added to the water to prevent them sticking together.

1. Place milk in pan with onion, carrot, celery, peppercorns and bay leaves

2. Add chopped peppers to minced beef, continue to cook for 5 mins

3. Fill the pasta sheets with the grated mozzarella and the beef mixture

4. Roll up the filled sheets. Place with joint side down in an ovenproof dish

5. Spoon or pour the freshly made sauce over the filled pasta to cover

6. Sprinkle top liberally with grated Parmesan cheese and cook until golden

SPAGHETTI BOLOGNESE

A tempting rich meaty tomato sauce with tasty vegetables, just a hint of wine and freshly chopped basil. Spaghetti Bolognese is probably one of Italy's best known and loved dishes.

Calories per portion: 297
SERVES 4

1. Prepare ingredients, wash celery, carrots, mushrooms. Peel, chop onion

2. Dry fry the minced beef over a gentle heat, stirring frequently until browned

3. Fry onion and bacon in the olive oil, then add remaining chopped vegetables

1 large onion
2 large sticks celery
2 large carrots
8 oz/225 g tomatoes
4 oz/100 g mushrooms
12 oz/350 g lean minced beef
2 oz/50 g back bacon
2 tbsp olive oil
¼ pint/150 ml dry white wine
½ pint/300 ml beef stock
1-2 tbsp tomato purée
salt and freshly ground
**   black pepper**
1 tbsp freshly chopped basil
12 oz/350 g spaghetti
freshly grated Parmesan cheese

Peel the onion and chop finely. Trim and wash celery, chop finely. Scrape or peel the carrots, trim and chop. Make a small cross in the top of each tomato, place in a bowl and cover with boiling water. Leave for 2 mins, drain, then peel and chop. Wash and dry mushrooms, chop.

Place the minced beef in a frying pan and dry fry over a gentle heat until browned. Stir frequently as this will help to break up the mince and keep the meat separate. When browned, drain through a colander to remove

any excess fat. Wipe the pan with absorbent paper.

Derind the bacon and cut into small strips. Heat the oil in the pan, then gently fry the bacon and chopped onion for 5 mins or until the onion is soft and transparent. Add the chopped celery and carrots and continue to fry for a further 3 mins.

Return the mince to the pan with the chopped tomatoes and mushrooms. Fry for a further 5 mins then pour in the wine and stock. Blend tomato purée with 2 tbsp of water and stir into pan, together with seasoning and the freshly chopped basil. Bring to the boil, then simmer gently for 35-45 mins or until the meat is cooked and the vegetables are tender but not mushy. Adjust seasoning.

Meanwhile, bring a large pan of lightly salted water to a rapid boil. Holding the spaghetti in a bundle, gently lower into the boiling water. As the spaghetti softens it will gradually curl around the pan. Cook for 10-12 mins or until it is 'al dente' (this is when the spaghetti is soft but still has a slightly chewy texture). Drain well. Mix the bolognese sauce into the cooked spaghetti and serve immediately with

freshly grated Parmesan cheese.

If you wish to cook the sauce in the microwave, place meat in a shallow dish and microwave on high (uncovered) for 5 mins. Drain off meat, reserve 3 tbsp of juices in dish. Add prepared vegetables, stir and microwave uncovered on high for 3 mins. Stir after 1½ mins. Return meat to dish with remaining sauce ingredients. Stir well. Cover and microwave on high for 10-12 mins or until sauce is thick.

If liked, you can include 4 oz/100 g chopped, cleaned chicken livers in the recipe – just add them to the mince when browning.

HANDY TIP

Pasta dishes which use spaghetti or tagliatelle need to be eaten immediately. Always serve in warmed dishes to help keep them hot.

4. Return the beef to the frying pan, then add the peeled chopped tomatoes

5. After adding the mushrooms to the pan, pour in the wine and then the stock

6. Bring a pan of lightly salted water to a rapid boil, slowly add spaghetti

LASAGNE

We've adopted some great classics from Italy and this is certainly one of them. This tasty dish is made from a rich meaty sauce, flavoured with tomatoes, garlic and basil, layered between pasta and topped with a cheese sauce.

Calories per portion: 522   SERVES 4

1 large onion
8 oz/225 g tomatoes
2 sticks celery
2 garlic cloves
12 oz/350 g lean minced beef
2 tbsp freshly chopped basil or
    2 tsp dried basil
salt and freshly ground
    black pepper
2 tbsp tomato purée
¼ pint/150 ml Chianti or red wine
¼ pint/150 ml beef stock
8-10 sheets pre-cooked lasagne
1½ oz/40 g butter or margarine
1½ oz/40 g plain flour
1 tsp mustard powder
½ pint/300 ml milk
3 oz/75 g mature Cheddar
    cheese, grated
1-2 tbsp Parmesan cheese, grated

Preheat oven to Gas 6, 400°F, 200°C, 15 mins before baking the lasagne. Peel onion and chop finely. Make a small cross in stalk end of tomatoes, cover with boiling water and leave for 2 mins. Drain. Peel tomatoes, then chop. Trim and wash celery, chop finely. Peel garlic and crush.

Place the beef with the onion, celery and garlic in a frying pan and fry over a moderate heat, stirring frequently until browned all over. Drain off any fat that may have run out while cooking. Stir in chopped tomatoes, basil, seasoning to taste, tomato purée, wine and stock. Bring to the boil, then simmer gently for 30 mins, stirring occasionally.

Place a layer of the minced beef mixture in the base of an oblong ovenproof dish. Cover with half the lasagne sheets. Top with remaining beef then cover with rest of lasagne.

To make the cheese sauce, melt the butter or margarine in a small saucepan, add the flour and the dried mustard, then cook for 2 mins. Draw off the heat and gradually stir in the milk. Return the pan to the heat and cook, stirring throughout until the sauce thickens and coats the back of a spoon. Add seasoning to taste and stir in the grated Cheddar cheese.

Beat until the cheese has melted, then pour over the lasagne, ensuring

that the pasta is completely covered. Sprinkle with the Parmesan, then cook in the oven for 25 mins or until the top is golden brown and bubbling.

1. Peel onion, leave root intact, chop finely. Blanch tomatoes in boiling water

2. Fry beef onion, celery, garlic, until beef is brown, and onion and celery soft

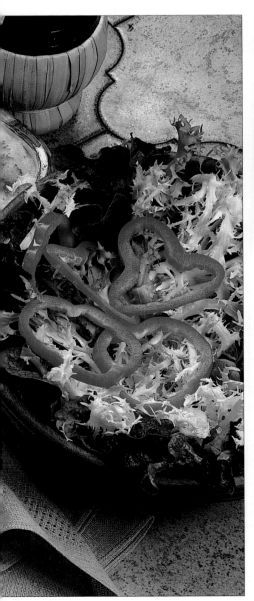

3. Add tomatoes, basil, seasoning, tomato purée, wine and stock, mix thoroughly

4. Place layer of cooked beef in ovenproof dish, cover with half the lasagne sheets

5. Make sauce, then add Cheddar cheese. Beat well to ensure smooth sauce

6. Cover last layer of lasagne with sauce, ensuring pasta is completely covered

ACKNOWLEDGEMENTS

All photography by John Elliott
Except for: Roast Stuffed Pork, Fish Casserole and Pasta with Basil by Karl Adamson
Chicken Marengo and Cassoulet by David Armstrong
Bacon in Cider by Bill Richmond

Gina Steer would like to thank Kathryn Hawkins and Jenny Brightman for their help in
assisting in some of the photography, styling and recipe testing.

MARY HOFFMAN has written over 90 books for children, that range from picture books to novels. *Amazing Grace*, first published in 1991, was commended for the Kate Greenaway Medal and has since become a modern classic. Together with its sequels, *Grace and Family, Princess Grace* and *Grace at Christmas*, and the storybooks *Starring Grace, Encore, Grace!* and *Bravo, Grace!*, it has sold over 1.5 million copies. Mary has also written the hugely successful *Great Big Book of Families*, illustrated by Ros Asquith, which is now in 15 editions worldwide. Her other books for Frances Lincoln include *The Colour of Home* and *Kings and Queens of the Bible*. She lives in Oxfordshire with her husband and three Burmese cats, and has three grown-up daughters, all working in the arts.

CORNELIUS VAN WRIGHT and **YING-HWA HU** have illustrated many children's books together, working in watercolour, including *Sam and the Lucky Money* and *I Told You I Could Play*. Their other books for Frances Lincoln are *Princess Grace* and *Grace at Christmas*, with Mary Hoffman. They live in New York City.